Bald on Top

Bald on Top

Bald on Top

A light-headed guide for the
Thinning, the Rugged – and the
just plain Bald!

James Whale

 Robson Books

First published in Great Britain in 1995 by Robson Books Ltd,
Bolsover House, 5-6 Clipstone Street, London W1P 8LE

British Library Cataloguing in Publication Data
A catalogue record for this title is available from the British Library

Book design by Harold King
Illustrations by Jim Hutchings

ISBN 0 86051 991 0

Typeset by The Harrington Consultancy
Printed in Great Britain by
St Edmundsbury Press Ltd, Bury St Edmunds, Suffolk

To my father, David,
a bald man amongst bald men

Contents

Acknowledgements

My grateful thanks go to John Bartlett, without whom this book would never have happened.

INTRODUCTION

*There is more felicity on the far side of baldness
than young men can possibly imagine.*
                                    Logan Pearsall Smith
                                    Afterthoughts (1931)

This is a book which is long overdue. I know this, largely
because I have several drawers full of letters from my
publishers telling me that it's overdue, but also because the
world is still, sadly, a place full of prejudice and almost as
full of people fighting it in its many forms.

Well, in nearly all its forms. The battles against racism,
sexism, heightism and many other 'isms' all have their
champions (and, in the case of the first two, even multi-
million pound industries built around them) and, whilst
some may argue, perhaps not unreasonably, that our battle
is not as important, it must be pointed out that the incidence
of baldism is far more widespread, is equally without
intelligent foundation and is directed against a greater
proportion of the population in the Western world than any
other form of prejudice.

If you doubt the last of those claims, examine the
statistics.

Roughly fifty per cent of all males over the age of fifty are
affected by the balding process and, although it may not be
widely known, the process starts for ninety-five per cent of
males by the time they reach that physical and emotional
time-bomb, puberty. Add to that the even less acknowledged
fact that the same parlous process also starts to affect the
hairline of seventy-five per cent of women, and we are
talking about the only form of prejudice which is practised
against the majority of the population!

In most women, of course, the balding process stops
almost as soon as it starts, which, by many people's
reckoning, is about the only physical advantage that the

ix

female of the species managed to secure when the various biological mechanisms and contrivances were being handed out. By *my* reckoning, of course, balding is no disadvantage but yet another in a long list of male advantages! I can only presume that Adam, being first in the queue, looked at what was on offer, picked out all the best bits for himself and wisely avoided all those other unpleasantnesses with which he knew man simply wouldn't cope. After all, it is widely accepted that had men been responsible for the actual process of childbirth rather than the infinitely more pleasant business of initiating it, the species would never have got off the ground. As for the biological cycle which enables the birth process, had that been visited upon men, it is quite likely that the effects of *male* PMT would have forced the development of some system whereby men would be forced into solitary confinement for the duration.

Throughout this book, the nature of the balding process is examined in the hope of making you aware, whatever the state of your own head, that balding is not only a perfectly natural state but also an eminently desirable one. Generally, the term 'bald' is used in fairly cavalier fashion (in view of the state of most Cavaliers' heads, possibly an inappropriate choice of term) and is intended to include all balding men whatever degree of baldness they may have achieved.

Obviously, the aspiration of us all should be the perfect, pristine, shining pate, utterly devoid of any hairy growth whatsoever but, sadly, that pinnacle of excellence is achieved by few of us. Receding hairlines (or, as it is better to call them, advancing headlines), fading crowns and thinning overall growth are all laudable steps on the great journey to baldness and each of them deserves the recognition of the generic term, 'bald'. Is a man with one hair on his head bald? This is a favourite topic with sixth-form debating societies (who spend a lot of time debating things about which their knowledge is, at best, skimpy.)

Later in this book various aspects of baldness will be illustrated from personal experience and from wide and extensive research (carried out in many and varied countries; Inland Revenue, please note) in order to help to persuade both the bald and the hirsute that baldness is not a cause for scorn or abuse.

Some of the lesser-known occurrences of baldness in early British history will be mentioned, together with some of the political implications; and regularly, and at some length, the advantages of the blessed state will be pondered. As an additional service to readers, some of the suggested alternatives to baldness (by way of cure or disguise) will be considered, and, having been considered, they will *quite objectively,* be rejected.

In short the three most effective weapons in the fight against prejudice in whatever form it may take – education, understanding and awareness – will be employed. Whether mathematics is *your* strong point or not, whether you are bald or hairy, there is something for you in this book.

Chapter 1

IN THE BEGINNING

*Bald (bo:ld) adj. 1. having no hair or fur, esp. having
no hair or fur on scalp. 2. lacking growth or covering.
3. a most desirable state.*

Whether you are bald or not, this is a book which can change your life by the simple expedient of changing your attitude to baldness.

If you are bald – on top, sides, front, back or even completely (the title is not meant to be exclusive) – this book will help you to understand that you are neither freak, rarity nor malformation. You are, in the words of the Good Book, a 'smooth man' not 'a hairy man' and you are in good company. John Milton, one of the finest poets ever to down a few pints of heavy on a Friday night, refers even to Adonis, that alleged pinnacle of male beauty, as 'smooth Adonis'. Contrast this with the names of those endowed with more than a normal complement of hair: Hitler, Stalin, Rasputin and so on. The list, as we shall see later, is almost endless.

If you are *not* bald, this book can educate you into a more understanding approach to baldness and may even set you on a lifetime quest for that blissful state.

The sad fact is that, at the moment, baldness gets a bad press. The public generally has an appallingly out-of-date attitude to it and, as is often the case with public hostility, this attitude is largely based on fear and ignorance. This has created a climate in which those who are bald feel, quite wrongly, that they are in some way underprivileged,

1

tonsorially challenged and, to some degree, lesser men as a result of a circumstance which is not only quite natural but also, as this book will show you, a highly desirable state.

Help is at hand – in fact, at this very moment, the instrument of that help is *in* your hand. The aim is to challenge current thinking on baldness. I shall start with you, and, once you have read this book, you will pass the word on (please don't pass the book on, but merely recommend it. We all have to earn a living!). The crusade will continue until, eventually, antagonistic attitudes to baldness will be as out of date as Dame Barbara Cartland's wardrobe and as rare as an honest politician.

Inevitably, before changing widely held attitudes, one has to start by understanding both why they are held and what is their effect.

Those lists which rank human experiences in order of their potential to cause stress almost always place (admittedly in differing sequences) death, divorce, moving house and supporting England's cricket team, in the top four positions. Take no notice. These lists are almost always compiled by people who are alive, single and living in the house in which they were born. (Sadly, we can offer neither hope for, nor explanation of, England cricket supporters.)

That their compilers share one other common factor is apparent from the lists themselves. At least, it is apparent from the constant omission of one particular experience. The compilers all, obviously, have a full head of hair.

One of the most stressful moments in human existence is the first moment at which the mirror reflects the onset of baldness. Not because it is horrific in itself, but because of the prevailing bias against it.

We are all supposed to remember where we were when we first heard the news of the deaths of Kennedy or Lennon (although much research has established that such claims rarely stand up to serious examination). The other event of which, according to legend, each of us remembers every

detail is his, or her, first sexual conquest (although, in our experience, it is more often that the individual concerned has no small difficulty in remembering even such a basic fact as the name of the other party involved – and this even in those cases where it was known in the first place!)

The claim of both of these events to memorial immortality pales into insignificance when put alongside the onset of baldness. Any of you reading this book in possession of a full head of hair (the rest will know it full well) may take it from me that the one moment which is engraved irremovably on the memory is that in which there was the first recognition of baldness.

In my case, it was a fine May morning. The sun dappled through the leaves of a brilliant yellow forsythia bush outside my bedroom. The pink and white blossom bursting from the apple tree in the garden was proof that burgeoning spring was giving way to a summer which would first produce and then ripen the fruits until that moment when the autumn gold would offer up her bounteous harvest. As I looked from my window, all was well with my world. It was a time of happiness, warmth, contentment and growth.

At least, it *was* in the garden!

I should have kept looking through the window. My eye strayed and chanced upon a mirror, and with that single glance, summer turned to winter in my eye.

More accurately, summer seemed to have turned to winter on the top of my head.

The shock was immense. I had never seen it before. I could say nothing. The words simply would not come. Until that moment, my life had been surrounded with hair, mostly people whose hair was shoulder-length or longer. I could not remember ever seeing anyone as bald as I looked in that mirror.

My mind instinctively grasped at the only available straw. Perhaps, by some chance, by some trick of angle or light, I had caught the reflection of someone else in the room, but no. It wasn't mother. It was me. I was bald.

Had I only been able to talk to someone about it then, I

suppose the experience would have been less traumatic. Had I had some close friend or confidante to whom I could confess my fears and worries, the memory might by now have paled. But I could not talk about it, I could not confide in anyone, I was alone and the mark of that moment is upon me to this day.

I was bald. My life was shattered – and I was only one week old!

Chapter 2

SCHOOLDAYS

Get yer 'air cut!

As far as is known (monastic orders, Hare Krishna communes and television game show hosts notwithstanding), baldness is neither infectious nor contagious. The incidence of violent crime is not manifestly higher amongst the bald. Bald men are no more prone to drive carelessly, drink heavily, spit in the street, beat their wives or dress in a manner likely to cause a breach of the peace. They are not malodorous, nor are they anti-social and, as far as we can discover, are not markedly more likely suddenly to remove their trousers in a public place and sing lewd songs in Basque dialect than any other human being.

In view of these indisputable assertions, is it not truly astounding that so much hostility and bias can exist against baldness? What is even more astounding is that this bias can exist in a society where for so many years the education system seemed to be dedicated to manifold, steadfast and various attempts at separating, in one way or another, young boys from their hair. Certainly this was the case during my days at school.

At that time, admittedly, the system had not yet come to terms with the fact that it was no longer necessary to prepare boys for National Service. Younger readers may not know that National Service was a systematic form of torture applied to professional soldiers, sailors and airmen, whereby they had to put up with the presence within their

ranks of the entire male population for two years of its late
adolescence. It was considered to be good experience for the
troops: if they could withstand the rigours of the National
Service intake, they were not likely to be frightened by
anything that the enemy could throw at them.

Fondly retaining the belief that their duty was still to
prepare boys for a 'kill or be killed' existence, the authorities,
accordingly, ran the education system on fairly militaristic
lines. No, I did not write 'run fairly on militaristic lines'.
Uniforms were still the norm at all levels of school (although
part of the game was to see how many pieces of uniform
could either be disguised by suitable amendment or even
completely abandoned without discovery) and a very clear
system of rank was established. The masters, naturally,
provided the 'officer class' (with a virtually complete ranking
system based on seniority and length of service), the Head
Boy was a sort of RSM (doomed never to be an officer but
rating himself a cut above the lower ranking officers) and
the rest of the prefects supplied the school with its
equivalent of the nastier breed of sadistic NCO to be found
in most branches of the services. The organization was so
similarly constructed to that of a regiment that, whilst it is
probably true that no pupil was ever actually shot for
revealing school secrets or court-martialled for letting chalk
fall into enemy hands, it is not really surprising that schools
almost universally shared the Army's horror of hair.

It has never been absolutely clear why the Army (or to a
lesser extent, the Air Force and Navy) has had such an
abiding hatred of hair. Indeed, for hundreds of years, long-
haired soldiers were the norm. It is ironic, then, that the
services should be so psychotic about the removal of hair in
a time when warfare has advanced (if 'advanced' be the
word) to the stage where, if the enemy is close enough to see
the length of your hair (let alone make contact with it),you
have already lost!

Since those days, of course, school standards have
changed – some might say disappeared, but education policy
is not the province of this tome – and whereas, in more

recent times, dependent upon contemporary fashion, it has been quite usual to see schoolboys wearing hair of a length greater than whatever had currently taken the place of the blazer, in those days close-cropped hair was the order of the day throughout the term.

As a result, as a matter of course, the school holidays provided a period in which hair was grown with an eagerness equal to that of any nurseryman producing roses for Chelsea Flower Show. All over the land could be heard the straining groans of boys trying to force their hair out from the inside as quickly as possible. Many went further and devised contraptions which would enable them to sleep with their heads resting in a mixture of John Innes No. 1 and peat. Along the grapevine would come the news of the latest growth-promoting discovery, and the corner grocer's shop would suddenly run out of (say) black treacle and arrowroot, or local chemists would have inexplicable queues of youths jostling for their diminishing stocks of copper sulphate and rose-water, for no reason which the owners of the premises could ever fathom.

The determination of boys to stimulate, in any way possible, the flourishing mane was not due *solely* to a desire to spend at least part of the holiday not looking like a fugitive from Alcatraz. It was also a necessary precaution for the ritual which would take place at the beginning of the next term and which was known as 'The Celebration of the first Communion of the Term between Master and Boy'. ('Communion' is used here in its more secular or temporal sense of 'an exchange of thoughts or emotions'.)

The prescribed procedure of this first encounter, as far as we are aware, has never before been formalized in any official text but it might as well have been. It seldom varied, and we are convinced that a form or forms of the text following must, at some time, have been promulgated at teacher training colleges throughout the land.

The Order of Service for the Occasion of the first Communion of the Term between Master and Boy

These exchanges may take place at any time and in any situation as may be, or be deemed by the Master to be, the first meeting between the Master and the Boy.

The Master and the Boy shall approach each other and the following shall be the form of words exchanged by them (the Boy shall speak first):

The Boy: Good Morning, Sir.
Master: Morning, (Boy's name).
The Boy: Did you enjoy your holiday, Sir?

Then shall the Master speak one of the following texts, as may be appropriate to the occasion:

Master: Thank you, (Boy's name), I did. Though I fear my holiday was somewhat like your hair.

or

Master: Unlike boys, (Boy's name), teachers do not have holidays. They simply work (if 'work' is a word within your ken) in a different place. The hours we travail, (Boy's name), are rather like your hair.

Here the Master may offer a chuckle at his own wit.

or

Master: Quite why you should entertain the concept that my holidays should be business of yours, (Boy's name), I fail to see. Which is, in all probability, what you will do very shortly.

or, if the Master be deaf, this:

Master: Quarter to nine, (Boy's name),

or, if the Master be deaf and short-sighted, this:

Master: Quarter to nine, (wrong Boy's name).

Whichever text is chosen by the Master, the Boy shall respond, quizzically:

The Boy: Sorry, Sir?

here shall the Master raise the forefinger of his right hand and jab sharply and repeatedly at the head of the Boy intoning:

Master: Too long, (Boy's name). Get it cut immediately.

and the Boy shall respond:

The Boy: Yes, Sir.

here shall the assembled congregation of 'other pupils' snigger, giggle and laugh in unison in order that the Master shall think he has re-established himself as one of the foremost wits of the century.

The Master and the Boys shall now proceed on their way.

After a few terms of taking part in this bizarre ritual, boys were often tempted to have their head shaved at the end of the school holiday in order to see if it would induce any variation in the order of service. As it happened, a classmate was ill one summer and suffered total hair loss. It made no difference at all. On the boy's first day back at school, his form master told him to get his hair cut. When the poor innocent lad pointed out that he had none left to cut, rather than receiving any expression of sympathy, he was punished for 'dumb insolence.' The old school charge of 'dumb insolence' was a forerunner of 'Catch 22' (later made famous by Joseph Heller in his book of the same name). If you didn't answer a master, you were booked for dumb insolence; if you did, you were booked for cheek.

The risk to hair didn't stop at that first encounter. There were other areas of school life which also took their toll.

'Aha!' you say. 'The dangers of the old chemistry labs? Steaming tubes and bubbling vats of foul-smelling, repellently coloured, viscous liquids of unknown evil intent, surpassed in their evil and malodorous vileness only by the daily output of the school kitchens?'

Sorry to disappoint you, but no. Apart from the odd disappearing eyebrow, occasional nasal hair and regular singeing of those on the back of the hand, the school labs were pretty free of depilatory dangers.

In one school, geography was the big danger. Or, more accurately, the geography master who, for reasons which will be revealed, was known simply as 'Hookey'.

Hookey was a pioneer. He was years ahead of his time. His pupils' wish was that he had been years ahead of theirs, too. In those dim and distant days, Hookey tried to do what Vidal Sassoon did so successfully some years later – part people from their hair. Vidal took a pride in it, raised it to an art form and simultaneously parted people from a substantial part of their wallets' contents. Hookey took pleasure rather than pride, raised it to a form of aggravated assault and was paid peanuts for it. However, more marked differences were to be observed in the methods and the results of each of them.

What Vidal achieved through subtlety, style and sheer skill, Hookey attempted with sadism, speed and brute force. Given the time, Vidal could produce a head which was a perfect tribute to style and craftsmanship. Given even less time, Hookey would probably have finished with a head that looked like an impression of a cat with alopecia. Fortunately, nobody gave him long enough to find out.

In all the years of Hookey's tender care, only one boy was slow enough to let the brute get away with more than one chunk of hair at a time – a rather puny unfortunate by the name of 'Poxy' Pocklington. Poxy was hampered by crutches, having broken his right leg in a fall and, having also broken his right wrist in the same fall, was additionally hampered by having enormous trouble mastering the use of the crutches. As a lasting tribute to the fear which Hookey's reputation instilled, even with Poxy impeded even as badly as this, Hookey only got two tufts.

Hookey always claimed to others (particularly to the headmaster and to visitors who were potential customers) to 'love the boys as if they were my own family, you know – each and every one of them', which is why he is not identified more closely here. It must have been embarrassing enough for his family to have had all its members spending their lives looking like a collection of threadbare rugs, without suffering the additional ignominy of being identified in this volume.

School playing fields were another immensely rich source of hair-removing exploits. In fact, such was the athletic and sporting prowess of schoolmates (and, it has to be said, of most of us) that far more hair was removed by brute force than was ever raised by deeds of derring-do. By the end of the rugby season, the heads of the forwards in our fifteens looked like flokati rugs which had been attacked by some gargantuan moth.

*

Although I have spent some time listing the danger areas in my schooldays, a time sometimes seemingly solely designed to separate young boys from their hair, I do so mainly to explain my considerable stupefaction at the bias against the bald which is held, astonishingly, largely by people who have also suffered the rigours of the same system.

I do not mean to imply that, in my case, the results of these attacks rendered my head less fully complemented than it might otherwise have been. Indeed, somewhat surprisingly (though on most occasions, more by judgement than luck), I avoided all the problems and dangers and survived my schooldays with a virtually full, if not exactly luxuriant, head of hair.

You can imagine then, my initial horror and my consequent complete exasperation only to survive all this, and then go bald immediately after I had escaped the dangers of school!

Chapter 3

Shining
THE ~~SWINGING~~ SIXTIES

The probability must be that most of those reading this book will either remember the 'Swinging Sixties' for themselves, or will have been bored rigid by the tales told about them by their elders. Either way, your view of the sixties is probably ripe for revision. Let us be honest, most of the decades and eras which have exciting sobriquets attached have earned them on fairly scant evidence and with hardly major effects on the population at large. The 'Naughty Nineties' (the 1890s, of course) weren't so much naughty as decidedly nasty for 98 per cent of the population; the 'Jazz Age' left even most of America untouched; the 'Roaring Twenties' were always more boring than roaring for the bulk of those families whose young men had been left on various blood-soaked mud patches throughout Europe a few years earlier. And, although this may conflict with either received legend or distorted memory, in truth, the 'Swinging Sixties' were actually 'swinging' for precious few of us.

The 'sixties' obviously implies a period of ten years, unarguably from 1 January 1960 to 31 December 1969, and anyone who thinks that the attributes claimed for the swinging sixties lasted throughout that period is badly mistaken. Indeed, some of them were hardly present at all. Admittedly, the decade had its moments. The Profumo scandal (a defence minister sharing a call girl with a Russian defence attaché when the Cold War was at its height) was, at least, a scandal worthy of the name – and certainly several streets ahead of some junior minister deciding to improve his jollies by wearing a Chelsea football shirt. What about the fashion revolution? What fashion revolution? It takes more than a mini-skirt and eyes like a panda to make a revolution. Of course fashion *changed*, because that's what fashion does – particularly in a nation which was still emerging from the deprivations caused by the war and whose population was still full of unfond memories of rationing.

In the world of music, the Beatles were undeniably a phenomenon, and probably one to never be repeated, but whenever tales are told of the great musical revolution of the sixties, it is well worth bearing in mind that, at the beginning of the decade, Britain's number one was 'What Do You Want To Make Those Eyes At Me For'? by Emile Ford and the Checkmates, and after the great musical revolution, the decade closed with Rolf Harris and 'Two Little Boys'. Interestingly, they both spent exactly 25 weeks in the charts, so it can hardly be argued that these were freak accidents of musical taste. As revolutions go, that could almost be the equivalent of uninventing the wheel!

Even some of the other widely acclaimed facets of the swinging sixties, the mini-skirt (then, as now, widely worn by women whose houses seemingly had no mirrors), the drugs, the 'overturning of social and political attitudes', all these were fairly geographically localized events and not parts of some changing national consensus. Outside London, you could have been forgiven for thinking that all this 'social revolution' was about as relevant to the average member of the population as Belgium is to – well, as Belgium is to anything really.

For me the sixties were years of unrest, instability and change. Not social, not international nor even professional. This was definitely personal. The instability was taking place on top of my head, as indeed was the unrest and change. In what I thought then was a cruel parody of Kipling, whilst all about me were not only keeping their hair but also growing it to ever-extended length, I was losing mine. Every year saw at least an inch or two added to the styles of those who were

held up as exemplars of fashion and every year saw me revealing yet more of the shining pate. That is why, for me, the decade will always be known as the 'shining sixties'.

I suppose that, had I been born ten years earlier, my hair loss would have started at a time when it would not have been noticeable. In the fifties, men's hair was worn short almost universally. To discover a receding hairline at the front (not to mention an 'advancing headline' at the rear) at a time when Vinny Jones's head would not have raised an eyebrow might not have made me feel like the outcast I undoubtedly did when those around me seemed intent upon being able to pass for yetis.

I started to disguise the onset of baldness as best I could. Cutting what remained very short, in order that the contrast would not be so great, merely resulted in getting abuse on two fronts. Wearing a cap worked for a while, but, before Donovan came on to the scene, looked ridiculous at any time other than winter. Looking at contemporary photographs now, I must admit that, on me, it looked fairly ridiculous even in winter. And, after Gilbert O'Sullivan came on to the scene, it provided yet another source of abuse.

There was no alternative, I just had to grin and bear it – and bare it! I decided to regard the hair which I had retained as a fitting surrounding to the glorious shining scalp it enclosed. After a while, I soon discovered that, as far as my immediate circle of friends was concerned, poking fun at Whaley's missing locks was a very short-lived pleasure. Every now and then, I ran into someone who I hadn't seen for a while and there would be a mild resurgence of mocking, but it became ever more rare. That set me thinking. Why worry? Just what was it that made people, me included, so ashamed of losing hair? Once the question is faced 'head on' (as it were), and you discover for yourself the utter illogicality of the scorn which a balding pate attracts (and then only for a short time), it becomes evident that, as there is no logical basis for the scorn, the scorn itself becomes irrelevant. Having worked that out, I can honestly say that I started to look at baldness much more constructively and, thus, this book and this attempt to make you think more constructively about it too.

Just as I refer to the decade in which I was first frightened, then exhilarated, by my advancing headline (more positive than 'receding hairline', you see?) as the 'shining sixties', so too will you soon start looking at the onset of baldness as your 'shining hour' and be able to consider all its advantages rather than being cowed by other people's negative opinions.

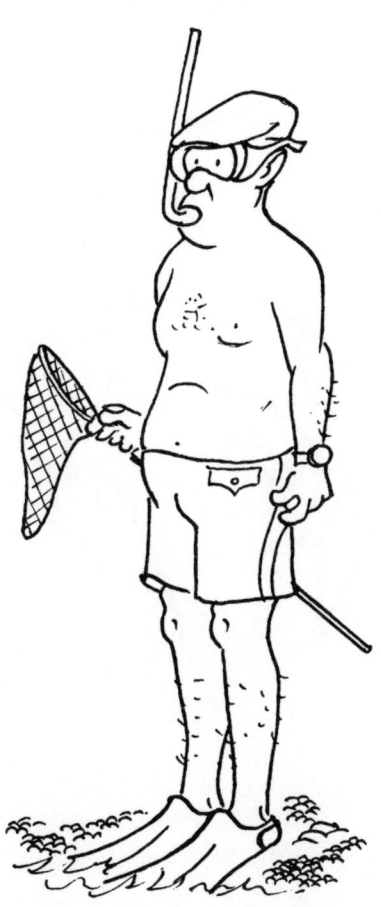

Chapter 4

BALDNESS ABUSE

Only the blind man laughs at the bald head.
Persian proverb

Each of you reading this book will have suffered abuse (I use the term 'abuse' in its general sense of 'verbal insult') of one sort or another during the course of your life. Those of you who are able to claim (honestly) that this is not the case should either get out more, or ring the author, who will be pleased to remedy the omission. Alternatively, most people will gladly help out, free of charge, if telephoned between the hours of four and five in the morning.

Whilst it is true that, in some ways, dealing with abuse arising out of your baldness is a similar process to the countering of abuse received for other reasons, there are differences which should be borne in mind – particularly by those of you desirous of staying in one piece.

The interesting question that is raised by the very existence of 'baldness abuse' is why baldness, almost alone amongst the physical features, is selected by adults as being 'fair game'? Children, of course, will pick on anything (or nothing) for poking fun at their peers, but when was the last time you heard an adult call someone 'Buck teeth', 'Cross-eyes', 'Jug-ears' or 'Big nose'? Yet 'Baldy' is still heard with amazing frequency.

Even whole conversational opening gambits built upon a person's baldness are (generally) regarded as socially acceptable. One could hardly believe that anyone would

21

open a conversation with, 'Hello! My you've got a lot of spots since I saw you last'. or, 'Of course I remember you – though you didn't wear thick glasses and a deaf aid in those days, did you?', or even, 'Yes, we were at school together, weren't we? (*Laugh*) Of course, you had both legs in those days!'

Of course not. All the examples quoted would generally be thought to be, at the very least, 'bad form' and would leave the speaker vulnerable, in some company, to open criticism and, in other company, to forming part of the internal ballast of a new motorway support pillar. Why then is baldness such a widely acceptable target? The reason is simple. The reason is also very important to our basic thesis that being bald is no reason for shame, humiliation or embarrassment.

As it is widely agreed that nobody but an unfeeling, bigoted fool would pour scorn on anyone with less than a full complement of legs, arms or other parts of the anatomy, and it is equally obvious that no such restraint is imposed by society upon gibes about those with less than the standard issue of hair, it follows that it must be subconsciously recognized by that same society that *there is no stigma, no disadvantage, and no problem in being bald.*

Look at the situation surrounding those whom the 'experts' would brand today as overweight. Some years ago, before everyone was expected to be thin as a lath, live on muesli with skimmed milk, and look like Jane Fonda or Kate Moss, there were lots of adults around nicknamed Tubby, Fatso, Barrel and even Jumbo. Where have they all gone now? Kidnapped, perhaps, by the Provisional Wing of West Harpenden Weight-Watchers? Eliminated, at the dead of night, by an active, rapid response snatch-and-kill unit of *Slimming Magazine*'s Liberation Front?

Look around you. The *people* are still there. It is only the nicknames which have vanished. I am aware, today, of only one person called Tubs, and, as he weighs in at a varying amount in excess of 24 stone, one might be forgiven for regarding 'Tubs' rather as an affectionate understatement than a term of abuse.

This has all come about as a result of a massive investment in making people think that 'thin is in', which in turn (or so it is intended) will then generate an even more massive income by selling them a vast range of foods, drinks equipment and videos which all, to one degree or another, promise them the means of rendering themselves down to proportions which, had they been left to their own devices, they wouldn't have wanted in the first place.

The flowing curve, the generous proportion, and an air of amplitude are all, now, *officially* out. It follows that to make remarks about people's possession of these characteristics is socially frowned upon. And yet, remarks about thinning hair and baldness are still acceptable. How can this be?

We repeat. It is subconsciously recognized by people that

there is no stigma, no disadvantage, and no problem in being bald.

Important though it may be, indeed *is*, to establish that fact firmly in mind, merely having done so, although it may explain the *acceptability* of such remarks, does nothing to answer all the problems caused by and the questions connected with what we shall call 'baldness abuse' – particularly for the 'abusee'.

Naturally, when confronted by an attack of baldness abuse, the abusee's first instinct is not to let it go unnoticed. I would be failing in my duty to my readers if I did not say at this point that letting it go unnoticed might well be the best option (and is almost always the safest!) But, if the remark has been noticed, this then raises the question of the nature and style of response. I unreservedly avow that a physical response is always ill advised, and also issue here a warning that before the question of *style* of response is answered, you would be well advised to consider the question of its *desirability*. At least, you would be well advised if you don't want people to laugh at your broken nose too.

The decision chart which appears on the next page may help you here. (Of course, it has to be admitted, that it is just as likely that it will not!)

TO RESPOND OR NOT?

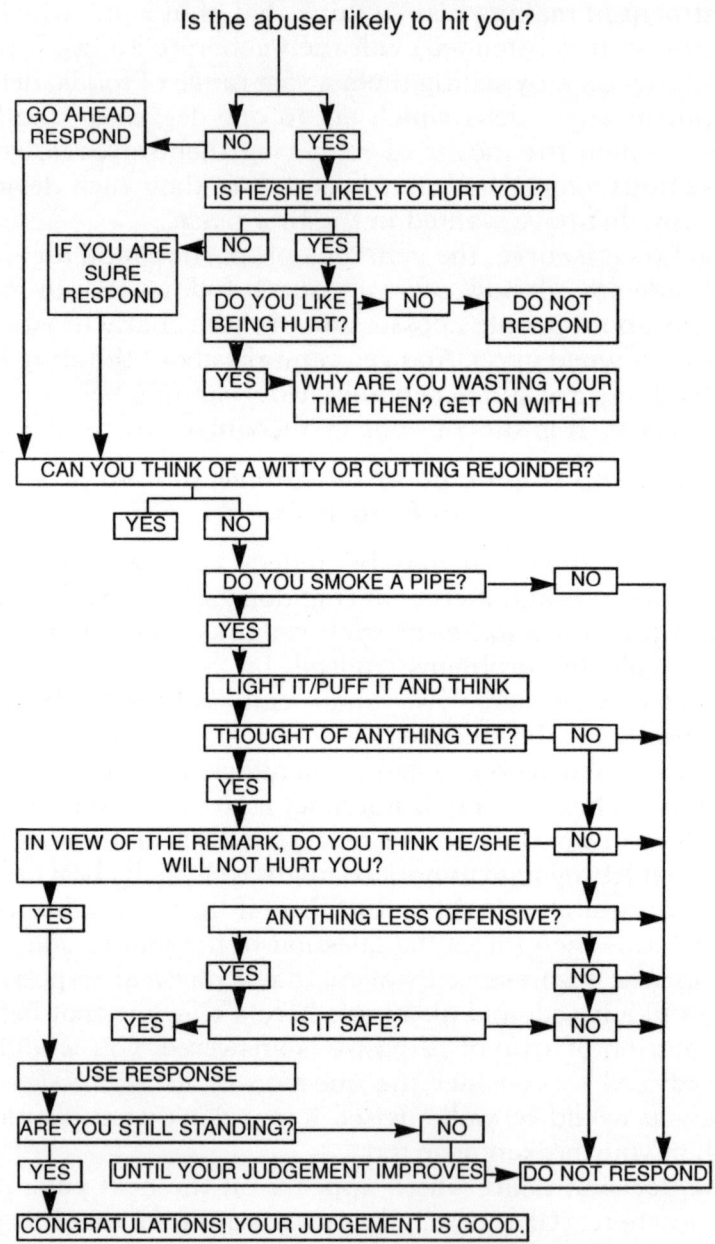

What may not help you is the realization that, 'in the field', you will have approximately two or three seconds in which to make your decision *and* frame your remark!

So, having consulted the chart on page 24, let us assume that you have decided that a response is both called for and, more importantly, prudent. What form should it take?

In selecting an appropriate response, so much depends on the style of abuse to which it is responding that consideration of some of the styles will be beneficial.

THE OPEN ABUSE APPROACH

If the abuse was of the charmless, blunt and openly hostile ('P--- off baldy!') school, a simple, 'No thank you' will normally suffice. It is unlikely that the abuser will have gained any standing or support amongst those present (other than from his probably similarly intellectually challenged colleagues) from such an attack, and so you hardly need feel obliged to respond in order to maintain your self-respect.

If fairly certain of your physical safety, you might venture a shade further with a 'Not just now thank you. I've only just had one.' This last response is particularly effective if delivered with a smile and will, of course, perform just as well as a response to a whole range of abusive suggestions with possible need to amend only the second part to something appropriate to the instruction. If you're *absolutely* certain of your physical safety, you can use the very patronizing, 'P...? That's an *awfully* big word for you, isn't it!', but no liability for the outcome is accepted.

Some of my favourite variations are the vague ('I never do before dinner'), the slightly hostile ('I don't think I'd risk it in present company'), and the obscure ('It's never a good idea in the close season, I find'). Obscurity is often a great asset in responding to abuse. It achieves automatically what a good response should always aim to do. It wrong-foots your opponent. He has to take time to work out just what you mean, and, by then, the moment is lost.

Indeed, if inspiration deserts you, an utterly meaningless remark may work quite adequately, as having no meaning, it is not possible for your antagonist to work it out.

Consider the following exchange, a friend, Ellis, used to his advantage in a crowded Gloucestershire pub:

> *Ellis:* Excuse me, I wonder if I might squeeze past?
> *Oaf:* Sod off, baldy.
> *Ellis:* Not just now thank you. Chickens never lay eggs before breakfast.
> *Oaf:* ??????????!

The oaf was so confused by this utterly meaningless remark that Ellis was easily able to make his way past to the gents in the resultant pause. Dangerous, but very effective when it works. (In fact, on Ellis's return, the oaf hit him, but that was an error of Ellis's subsequent judgement and not of his response selection technique.)

There is another (relatively minor) danger in this in that overuse of the 'meaningless remark technique' will result in your being regarded by all and sundry as a raving idiot.

THE OUTWARDLY FRIENDLY

This is the 'Hello, old boy! It must be very cold being that thin on top in this weather' sort of thing – and, annoyingly, always said with an air of originality which might have been appropriate for Oscar Wilde or Noël Coward at their best but which here is wholly misplaced. The trouble with this one is the very friendliness of it. Making a really crushing response is very definitely overkill which will gain sympathy for your abuser, and, therefore, the secret here is the light touch. Firstly, agree, and then make whatever response you choose in a very, very-light-hearted way, preferably with a laugh before and after it.

(Laugh) Yes, freezing, but at least that's better than being empty inside all year round. *(Laugh)*

THE SUBTLE SARCASM

This is a difficult one. It is widely heard that 'sarcasm is the lowest form of wit', though, normally, people who say this are those who cannot think of an answer. Sarcasm *can* be the lowest form of wit, but it is by no means always so. Indeed, in the right brain, sarcasm can be one of the most incisive tools in the armoury. Far from being abuse, a finely honed piece of sarcasm can scale considerable heights of the use of language. It is less likely to rise to such vertiginous heights in the context of baldness but it can be very effective, particularly when delivered with the appearance of a light touch. 'Wearing away on top a bit, then? Let's hope it's the only on the outside, eh?', or, 'Despite your outward appearance, old bean, I'd never had you marked down as an egghead.'

Such remarks are difficult to counter when you first hear them, and much enjoyed by bystanders who are always ready to appreciate a talent for the witty ad lib. Therein lies the rationale of your response. Why do you think it *is* an ad lib? Only because *they*'ve never heard it before. Even if it is an ad lib, there is nothing to stop you casting doubt on the fact – but with an equally light touch and a shared appreciation of the brilliance of the remark.

'That's very good, George. *(Pause)*Where did you read that one?' Or even, rather more dismissively, 'You always were one of the best-read men I've known.' This, with a knowing smile implying that it is really only the two of you who recognize the quote, can be very effective. George cannot simply return with a hurt, 'I made it up!', because he knows it will sound like a lame attempt to disguise his having been found out.

Now that George is wrong-footed, you can hit home further if you wish, with a disparaging remark about some aspect of George. For example, in the (possibly unlikely) event of George's being a writer or a journalist, you can strike gold with, 'Though not, it must be said, one of the most *widely* read men I've known.'

If nothing appropriate to George springs quickly to mind (and speed is the essence) you can always fall back on, 'If you had a pound for each time you've said that, I bet you'd buy a round!' After this, for George to prolong the exchange will simply look like a fit of pique. (Avoid the traditional rejoinder about grass never growing on busy streets because it may well be pointed out in return that it doesn't grow on concrete either.)

Obviously, whether you respond or not, you may always console yourself with the well known fact, that in the vast majority of instances, abusive remarks stem from the jealousy of the abuser towards the abusee, and so it is here. Keep reminding yourself that these sad, sorry fellows are generally covetous of your gleaming pate, envious of your shining crown, and tell yourself that, perhaps, after all is said and done, you really do not want to add to the sum of their misery by a crushing *bon mot*. It is particularly useful to keep reminding yourself of this on those occasions when a crushing *bon mot* does not actually come to mind.

5 things you may be called ...

1 Baldy

2 Slap-head

3 Suedehead

4 Cueball

5 Bonedome

... and 5 (rather more articulate) responses

1 I've seen better hair-styles than yours on the arse of an elephant.

2 Well, nobody could accuse you of being two-faced because you sure wouldn't choose to wear that one.

3 If an original thought ever struck you, you'd be concussed for a month.

4 It's just as well you don't have to live by those wits.

5 You're about as interesting as *one* boxer.

Chapter 5

TWO EXPLODABLE MYTHS

Man is a mammal; mammals have hair;
therefore it is more natural for men
to have a full head of hair than to be bald.

So just what is supposed to be so *natural* about hair?

Ah, you say, man is a mammal. Those slender growths emanating from the epidermis termed 'hair' are the characteristic covering of the mammal. Therefore it is natural for man to have hair. This is false logic and, in fact, this style of false logic can best be termed 'jumped logic' because it moves from one proposition to another by leaping over facts which would otherwise get in the way. (Students of party political broadcasts will be well aware of it.) Although such a proposition may appear reliable at first glance, further examination identifies it as being just about as sound (and as useful) as a chocolate kettle. The falsity of 'jump logic' can be more obviously demonstrated by a couple of similarly constructed, but more evidently incorrect, statements.

Consider the following two propositions (both based on 'jump logic'):

   a. All chickens are born in a shell, therefore anything sold to you without a shell is not a chicken.

   b. All mice are born blind, therefore the fact that a farmer's wife can cut off the tails of three of them

with a carving knife is hardly surprising, let alone
worth immortalizing in a nursery rhyme.

Few people would find themselves agreeing with either a or
b because they are so palpably ludicrous. Actually, the very
thing that makes them ludicrous is the very same thing that
makes our 'Explodable Myth 1' ludicrous – namely, the
passage of time. Just because *at some time* chickens are in
the shell and *at some time* mice are blind, we do not expect
either of them to remain in the same state. So too with
mammals. The characteristic of the mammal is that *at some
time* it has hair.

When was the last time you saw a shaggy elephant? (It is
just possible that older readers may remember the
mammoth, but unlikely.) Or a rhinoceros with ringlets? Or
even an armadillo sporting dreadlocks? Whales and
manatees have hair only at the embryonic stage. So why
should it be presumed that man, merely on the flimsy
foundation that he is a mammal, should spend his *entire* life
with a head coated in the ineffectual stuff? Why has there
been the continuance of the belief that every normal human
being should not only have great swaths of hirsute
embellishment but should also, as a result, be saddled with
meeting a larger amount for its lifetime maintenance than
would be paid over the same period of time for the same
length of a motorway?

If we go back far enough along the human being's family
tree – say, roughly to the point where he was still living in it
– we can see that there was at that time a purpose in this
follicled frenzy. Though any illness suffered as a
consequence of such an experiment must be your own
responsiblity, if you have any doubts, just try sitting stark
naked half-way up a tree in the middle of nowhere on a
freezing cold night with a nasty old wind blowing across
from the Urals, and you will soon see why only the hairier
amongst the species would survive.

Had the process of natural selection been left to itself, it
would, in turn, tend to mean that the hairier families would

have been more likely to breed successfully and thus establish even more strongly the continuance of long lines of primitive Man with overall body hair in amounts which would do credit to the inside of a Victorian sofa.

Is anyone seriously going to suggest that, today, possession of hair in such quantity would be regarded as a sign of civilization?

I trust that we may all agree that, over the millennia, *Homo sapiens* has evolved. Not yet, perhaps, quite *sapiens* enough to realize that Jonathan Ross is but Terry Wogan with a speech impediment, but certainly *sapiens* enough to know the difference between wearing a coat and growing your own.

The fact is that, as Man became more civilized, so his evolutionary pattern determined that what had once been essential (when keeping the icy blasts from doing their worst in the wide open spaces), was no longer quite as necessary (whilst in the comparatively unexposed surroundings encountered in wheeling a trolley around Tesco's). Interestingly, social scientists are currently investigating a theory that a roll of protective fat around the shin is evolving to counter the blows received in this very process.

If, then, we accept that the minimization of body hair is part of the evolutionary process through which Man has progressed in his civilization, is it not logical to accept, similarly, that the minimization of body hair in the region of the head is just part of the same process?

If you have followed the logic of this argument, then you will come to understand that the unavoidable conclusion is that bald men are *more* civilized, and *further* along the evolutionary chain, than their more fleecy fellows.

Explodable Myth 1 therefore explodes and is replaced by:

Reality 1
Bald men are more civilized than hairy men.

Explodable Myth 2
Hair = Power = Virility

I always suspected that the above equation would look quite absurd in print. It is quite a relief to discover that I was right. In fact, you may even be tempted to skip this interruption, but I would urge you not to because behind the obvious inequality is a wealth of fallacy and a world of insinuation which is only too familiar to those acquainted with baldness.

There is, undoubtedly, a proportion of the general public which regards an abundance of hair as a sign of virility and masculinity. It would be interesting, but expensive, to undertake research to establish the average IQ of such people. Our (unresearched, but much cheaper) guess is that the average IQ may well run into double figures – if only just – and possibly only on a good day at that!

On what can this extraordinary connection between hair and virility be based? My theory is that it may well have its roots in the legend of the famous, bad tempered Old Testament vandal, Samson, so a closer examination of his legend may yield worthwhile results.

Samson is a Hebrew name meaning 'child of the sun-god' or 'sunny one' (most ill-fitting when you consider the behavioural problems which reveal themselves in the later stages of his career). Samson is forever famous for two things: his hair and feats of strength. Not, you may think, the greatest legacy to humanity and he certainly is not remembered for any great feats of intellect!

Legend has it that Samson was born of the barren wife of Manoah of Zorah after the intervention of an angel, but, as is quite customary in this sort of case, little consideration seems to be given to the idea that it may well have been Manoah of Zorah that was deficient in the procreative area and that the 'angel' was more likely to be some other inhabitant of Zorah, blessed with rather more effective procreative equipment.

The angel apparently dictated that no razor should ever touch the boy's head (always very strong on illogical constraints, angels) and it was supposedly through his hair that Samson was endowed with the supernatural strength which enabled him to perform his great (if factually somewhat dubious) feats – strangling a lion and slaying a thousand Philistines with the jawbone of an ass being two of the more notable (and dubious).

Well, call me cynical if you wish, but honestly, though there may have been some pretty odd infantry achievements over the years, killing a thousand Philistines with the jawbone of an ass takes a bit of beating, surely? Were it true, it seems extraordinary that the story of David and Goliath even rated a mention. However, let us take it, for the moment, at face value and see what happens next. We then have this hirsute, hallowed hero behaving like your average Tory MP. He falls for a woman, Delilah, who manages to shave his head, reduce him to seven-stone-weakling status and hand him over to the Philistines (of whom, you will remember, he had personally slain a thousand). No sooner do they get hold of this mass murderer than they content themselves with merely putting out his eyes (by the reported standards of the time, we can only presume that to be the Philistine equivalent of a hundred hours of community service) and then the silly buggers let him grow his hair back! As a result of this, the (now blinded) bruiser then manages to 'pull down' the pillars of a building big enough to hold another *three thousand* of the Philistine fools – and, this time, without the aid of as much as the fibula of a hamster, let alone the jawbone of an ass.

So, on this extraordinary myth is based the other: that hair is a sign of virility. Well, you may subscribe to this if you will, but I won't. As is mentioned elsewhere (where I deal with the physiological background to baldness) the virility myth is not supported by medical knowledge, either. Excess testosterone, which *can* be linked to aggression (and which Samson must have been churning out in greater quantities than the brown stuff coming out of the Coca-Cola Corporation) can lead, if it leads to anything, to advancing baldness, but not to hair in the quantities which the so-called 'sunny one' is reputed to have had.

And so, in place of a myth, once again, we offer you a reality:

Reality 2

Bald men are just as masculine and virile as their less favoured hairy counterparts.

Chapter 6

THE BORING BIT

Somewhere in a book of this nature there is bound to be chapter devoted to the real facts which lie beneath the surface of the subject and this is it. You may wish to ignore it, but I advise you to give it a try.

Let us look closely, for a moment, at that oft-encountered but oxymoronic phrase, 'a healthy head of hair'. (Oxymoronic? In this case 'oxy–', meaning with the brains of an ox; '–moronic', meaning moronic.)

Those of us with a gleaming, well-polished pate devoid of scurf, dandruff and other manifestations which hair is heir to, must declare at the outset that, to us, nothing can be more attractive, healthy and beneficial. However, in an effort to remain at least a little objective, I must also acknowledge that so many people have fallen victim to the propaganda (often perpetrated by those with vested interests) in favour of the concept of 'a healthy head of hair' that some time must be taken to examine the medical background to hair – what it is, what it does and how it does it.

WHAT IS HAIR?

Hair is an outgrowth of the epidermis of mammals. Only mammals can have real hair, and all mammals do, as we have mentioned before, *at some stage in their development*. From the truly shaggy, such as the yak, to the apparently hairless such as the armadillo, there are no exceptions. It is true that some mammals (such as the whale and manatee) have advanced to a stage that, realizing the utter pointlessness of hair to their existence, they shed it very early, but, while we may look forward to mankind's reaching that stage in the fullness of time, at present it is only we, the chosen ones, who are showing the path to enlightenment.

HAIR STRUCTURE

Hair is made up of a fibrous protein called *keratin* (also involved in the formation of skin and nails), which is itself composed of nasty-sounding things like sulphur and amino acids. As if that were not revolting enough, there is worse to come. All hair you can see is made up of this keratin stuff and *dead cells*. Despite the appalling thought of all this dead matter hanging off the top of your head, it makes sense for these to be dead cells, of course, because otherwise the effect of asking the barber for a 'quick trim and not much off the top, please' would be the equivalent in pain value of nipping into the wood-cutting department of your local DIY store and asking for 'just the fingers but not much off the thumbs, please'.

The root of the hair, a sort of bulb-like contraption, grows in a hole called the *follicle*, which is the living bit and which always remains under the scalp. This has to be supplied with water, minerals, vitamins (and heaven knows what else) to keep it going by blood vessels called capillaries, and they have also got their work cut out disposing of all the waste products (yes even follicles do it!) by dumping them into the lymph system. Yet another gadget called the *sebaceous gland* apparently secretes oil which it has to supply to the follicle in order to nourish it. Even the base of the hair shaft itself is a complex chappie, having three different layers doing different jobs.

All this, so that Man can have great tufts of dead stuff hanging about his head. It almost defies belief.

Just imagine the amount of effort which is required of a body to keep all that going throughout the course of a lifespan. Although we are not content to make any meaningful evaluation of the specific workload which this may add to the body, in terms of return for effort expended, it must be comparable with breakfast television. One glance at the illustration of the process may be enough for any but the least squeamish.

HAIR GROWTH

The average head can boast (?) approximately 120,000 hairs. The range, however, is enormous: Though there are other variations affected by colour and race, redheads seem to cope with as few as 90,000 of the more coarse examples; blondes with around 150,000 finer specimens. If in doubt whether an alleged blonde is 'real' or 'artificial', you could set about counting the hairs on the head, but there are other more interesting and less time-consuming methods available which lie outside the scope of this volume.

It is widely recognized that hair patterns (quantity, colour, baldness rate and so on) are determined almost at conception, and throughout our lives hair is constantly renewing itself (or not) at various rates determined by our genes.

There are three main types of hair: *lanugo*, which is the downy fleece which covers us all in the womb and which we all have the wit, even at that early age, to ditch just before emerging into the world; *vellus hair*, the fine short stuff which covers most of us; and the rather gruesomely named *terminal hair* which sprouts on heads, eyelashes and eyebrows. That awesome process, puberty, triggers the growth of terminal hair in armpits, pubic regions and on the faces of men (well, mostly men!) Interestingly, if somewhat paradoxically, puberty, whilst doling out greater or lesser dollops of the stuff in all those, largely unnecessary, areas, is also responsible for the simultaneous receding of the hair at the temples. This process affects some 95 per cent of boys and even 75 per cent of girls. In years to come, the medical profession of *Homo sapiens plus* (or whatever succeeds us) may look back on all this as just another stage in the evolutionary process on the way to puberty's ultimately entailing the loss of all hair, but not before *Homo sapiens* finally wises up to the complete lack of any need for it in the modern world.

LIFE CYCLE

We should all get through something like twenty-odd cycles of hair growth in a lifetime – give or take the unanticipated, and unseen, oncoming bus. The simple view of hair's life cycle is fairly straightforward and somewhat similar to employment patterns: growth, a period of between three and six years, and rest, when the dead hair has a breather for three months or so and waits to be pushed out by a new arrival. As the number of cycles is pre-determined, it follows that the shorter the length of the growth period, the more quickly will you achieve the much to be desired state of baldness.

HAIR LOSS

Trichologists, who are 'those specializing in that branch of medicine dealing with hair *and diseases* of the hair' – obviously, it follows that no hair = no disease of the hair, – like all tradesmen, professionals and others with an eye to the contents of your wallet, have a wealth of technical terms for the different sorts of hair loss *Alopecia* – that's one for starters: all hair loss appears to be technically termed alopecia, a word derived, quite maliciously, from the Greek word for *mange in foxes*! Broadly, two types of hair loss appear to be identified: physiological and pathological. Physiological is regarded as natural or normal hair loss, whilst pathological hair loss is regarded as due to abnormal factors such as malnutrition, disease, stress and so on. Strangely, *Beadle-drop*, the condition suffered by those reduced to tearing out quantities of their own hair as a result of over-exposure to certain television presenters, appears not to be medically recognized.

The first, and possibly most natural, form of hair loss is the loss of that downy-like stuff, the *lanugo*, by newborn infants. The next most frequent is that which the experts refer to as male pattern baldness (although, as it affects women as well, only the 'experts' know why it is referred to as 'male'!)

MALE PATTERN BALDNESS (MPB)

Male pattern baldness (or, if the experts want to sound unchallengeably authoritative, *androgenic alopecia*) can affect men or women and is a genetic condition which is entirely natural – we'll say that again:

which is entirely natural.

In Western races, MPB affects roughly 30 per cent of males by the age of thirty, 40 per cent by the age of forty and 50 per cent by the age of fifty, so it would seem to be even hardly a matter for comment, let alone all the abuse and opprobrium with which it is sometimes greeted. Some other races are not as fortunate and do not have the Westerner's balding advantages. Easterners (by whom I mean Orientals, not those coming from Norfolk and Essex, whose rates of baldness seem to differ little from those in Dyfed or Cornwall), American Indians, most Mexicans and a lot of Africans have extremely low chances of reaching the blessed state through MPB.

MPB is affected by hormones ('What isn't these days?' you cry), notably androgen (a.k.a. that hate-figure of the feminist movement, *testosterone*, responsible, it is alleged, for every bad thing from war and famine to the late running of the

08.33 from Macclesfield). Though present in males and females, androgen is far more prevalent in the male.

Experts claim (you may think you detect some scepticism creeping in here) that androgen is responsible for such 'typical male characteristics' as coarse, thick facial hair, aggression and baldness. (Strange, you might think, then that this lowly hormone rarely seems to receive the equivalent credit for patience, promptness or the ability to drive a car through a gap two feet wider on either side without scratching the wing, but who said life was fair?)

There actually exists an acknowledged, eight-stage scale (the Hamilton scale) identifying the process of MPB, but there is a limit on how boring we are prepared to be – even in the boring bit! It follows a fairly regularly established pattern. First the receding at the temples; then thinner above the forehead; the bald patch on the crown which develops until a diminishing line of hair trails around the side and back of the head in a horseshoe shape. (In my view, it is not mere coincidence that the horseshoe has been a symbol of good luck in Western societies for centuries – though the fact that Nelson had one nailed to the mast of *Victory* may cast doubt on its efficacy!)

Whatever the causes, and I have stated that the entire process is pre-determined for each individual by genetic make-up, it must be said again that, whatever scientific mumbo-jumbo scientists may devise when talking about it, even they have to agree that

baldness is entirely natural.

Self-improvement task

Learn needlecraft and embroider a sampler with the words:

BALDNESS IS <u>ENTIRELY</u> NATURAL

---

10 things you're less likely to get if you are bald

1 Dandruff.

2 Scurf.

3 Lice.

4 Alopecia areata. (With or without parmesan and extra garlic)

5 Seborrhoeic dermatitis.

6 Premature greying.

7 Split ends.

8 Falling hair.

9 Your hair ruffled 'affectionately' by unfavourite female relatives.

10 Conned into parting with great wads of the folding stuff by a haircare industry trying to persuade you to make the contents of your bathroom shelves read like the contents of the fruit section of Fortnum and Mason's.

Isn't that a comforting thought?

Chapter 7

CURES – AND WHY YOU SHOULD AVOID THEM

> *You can expect to pay up to £5,000 for hair surgery and there is a certain amount of discomfort involved.*
>
> Liz Earle
> *Quick Guides: Hair Loss*
> (Boxtree, 1995)

By now, of course, you should be well aware why you should be properly sceptical of anything claiming to 'cure' baldness. Baldness is not a disease and therefore does not require a 'cure'. All it requires is the knowledge that it is not only a perfectly natural state, but also to be admired, enjoyed and thankful for.

In addition there is something else of which you should be aware:

there is no miraculous cure for baldness.

In this chapter I am using the terms 'bald' and 'baldness' to refer to normal male pattern baldness or MPB. I fully accept that for other types of baldness, such as some forms of pathological baldness, treatment *by properly qualified personnel* has made enormous advances and can have extremely successful results.

There are various methods which claim to retard the balding process and which indeed do seem to have some success (if 'success' is the word for such a dubious action). It is equally true that this branch of 'medicine' attracts more than its fair share of charlatans, cheats, knaves, conmen, swindlers, tricksters, frauds, impostors and bamboozlers. Beguiling though they may be, if you should decide, for whatever strange and perverse reasons of your own, to try to reduce your advancement to the burnished bliss of baldness, watch out for the quacks because, rest assured, they will certainly be watching out for you.

We have all seen the advertisements: two photographs, one an attractively bald man, though normally wearing an expression which might be appropriate had he just been told that the wrong leg has been amputated, the other, the same man transformed into a happy buffoon with an idiot grin and, so it would appear, completely oblivious of the fact that he seems to have a dead gerbil on his head.

Let me reiterate, if only for legal reasons, that there are treatments which do seem to have some success in their efforts to minimize the rate of hair loss and there are other treatments (see below) which will redistribute what hair you do have to attempt an appearance of new growth. Some of both types are discussed here, but the list is almost endless and constantly changing as new methods of restoring hair and reducing your bank balance are claimed to have been discovered. (Wigs, toupees and hairpieces are dealt with in a different chapter.)

DRUGS

Possibly the most effective of drug treatments currently available is *minoxidil*. It is somewhat unusual for an 'anti-baldness' drug in that it is not hormone-based. It is sold (on prescription) as a lotion called Regaine (which I presume has more to do with the influence of marketing men than lack of spelling ability on the part of the manufacturers) and, like all the best medical discoveries, was discovered almost by accident. It was, in its earlier career, available on

SURGERY RECEPTION

MINOX IDIL

prescription as an oral treatment for blood pressure. I have not researched its efficacy with regard to blood pressure but have no reason to assume it was other than effective. Sadly, it also had a tendency in some patients to be side-effective as well. Hair started growing in places which were not traditionally associated with the stuff: forehead, cheeks, and so on. With a laudable degree of lateral thinking (or marketing strategy), victory was snatched from the jaws of defeat and trials established that the *application* of minoxidil (as opposed to its ingestion – please be very clear about the difference if you try it!) did have an arresting affect on MPB. It has a success rate of somewhere between five and twenty-five per cent and is better on a bald patch than on an advancing headline (known, typically pessimistically, to the trade as a receding hairline). You will have to apply it twice a day and, if you stop, you are likely to be back where you started after about three to six weeks. It *is* a drug, available on prescription only, and all drugs can have side-effects. (As this was how the thing was discovered to be useful, in this case it hardly needs stating!)

Oestrogen cream was, at one time, a popular application treatment. Indeed, at one time, it was actually ingested by men as a treatment for hair loss, but the development of female sex characteristics in some of them didn't do a lot for its popularity, and so it has recently lost ground. It has to be applied daily and for ever.

THE 'WEAVE'

It is somewhat remarkable that this technique ever became popular in the first place. It is a method of weaving artificial hair in with your own to make it look as though you have more.

Sounds simple? Well it is really – until you remember that your real hair on to which it is woven is growing all the time. Therefore, unless you want your head to resemble a sort of weirdly fringed lampshade and have everyone singing

'Surrey With A Fringe On Top' whenever you appear, you have to go in for a service periodically to have the hair moved back to its original position. (Didn't they think of this when they started?)

SURGERY

Most experts will agree that for MPB surgery in one of the various forms is the only treatment which will last. As all forms of hair-replacement surgery involve transplant, and nobody has yet started donor arrangements or hair-banks, it follows that you have to have some of the stuff, and in sufficient quantity, somewhere on your head from which it can be taken. According to one expert, 'You can expect to pay up to £5,000 for hair surgery and there is a certain amount of discomfort involved.' (Frankly, that 'certain amount of discomfort' would put me off, even if it were not a contender for Understatement of the Year Award, but do read on if you are still tempted.)

Punch grafting
Punch grafting is possibly the most often encountered type of surgery currently in use. It involves taking small bits of your head (OK, bits of the scalp, but it amounts to the same thing) from areas where there is hair and moving them to bits of your head where there isn't, and will result in about three per cent of your original allocation of hair reappearing. (*Three* per cent: that's about 3,600 hairs. Big deal!) This is the one that can tend to give people (particularly certain television personalities) the appearance of that of a victim of a particularly violent spud-gun attack to the head.

Scalp reduction
The words 'Scalp reduction' sound nasty when you first hear them but, on further investigation, the actual process involved in scalp reduction appears to be far nastier than the

words ever sounded before you investigated them.

In this one a patch of your bald spot is sliced off and the remaining edges of skin are pulled together! If necessary, the process will be repeated, though its proponents will probably stop some way short of the time when your ears appear side by side on the top of your head.

Flap grafting

Flap grafting (do have a fairly large bowl placed nearby before you start reading this bit) is a skin graft by any other name.

A piece of your head with hair on it is grafted on to a piece of your head without hair on it. It is another idea that sounds awfully simple, and it also sounds simply awful, come to think of it – which I'd rather not. Could a similar effect not be obtained by supergluing a hairpiece to the bald area? It's fairly certain that a similar amount of pain could be experienced by then ripping it off again.

Others

As I mentioned earlier, the list is almost endless and ever-growing, but there is one more process that might usefully be brought to your notice.

Do you remember the name of Andy Bryant? 'Yes,' you say, 'I remember the name of Andy Bryant. How could I forget it? You've only just told me; it's Andy Bryant.'

Don't be facetious. Whether you remember him or not, you will almost certainly remember what he did. He was the brave (or foolhardy) soul who underwent a vasectomy under hypnosis. Admittedly, this is a whole lot more impressive than anything you are likely to see on the Paul McKenna television hypnosis show, but as to whether it makes Andy Bryant more or less likely to become a figure of influence to you is obviously your decision.

Anyway, Andy, who has been losing hair for some time (presumably hypnosis is less than helpful in this regard), was not at all happy with the usual reasons advanced for, and approaches to, baldness, so he undertook some ten

years of his own research. He has come with what might be
termed a holistic approach. His answer is the Natural Hair
Products programme* (NHP) which comprises **SIDES**, a
mnemonic for **S**tress – **I**nversion – **D**iet – **E**xercise –
Shampoo and which claims significant results.

To combat **Stress** (which, apparently constricts your
blood vessels and, presumably, mucks up all that capillary
action we referred to in 'The Boring Bit' earlier), NHP
recommends, among other things, setting yourself a five-
year plan for relationships, finance and work. (It is your
decision whether you think that drawing up the plan itself,
or any failure to meet its aims during the five years, is likely
to cause you more stress than it relieves.) In order to see
how you are getting along on the stress front, you will also
get (for a consideration) a little plastic gizmo to stick
on your arm and monitor your stress levels (and possibly
serve as a conversation piece in duller moments). NHP will
also let you have (for a consideration) tapes to combat
stress.

Diet (I'll get to inversion in a minute) is heavy on fruit and
veg, at least eight glasses of water a day, and ease off on the
coffee and alcohol fronts (nothing terribly revolutionary
there then).

Exercise is a mixture of special scalp exercises and an
exhortation to exercise more in general to reduce tension.

Your **Shampoo** should be as close as possible to the
natural pH factor of the scalp (normally 5.0 – 5.6, but I'm
not sure whether you get a plastic gizmo to measure
this, but you can order a special shampoo – for a consideration).

Finally, what you have been waiting for: **Inversion**. In
normal English, as you will be aware, 'inversion' means
either turning upside down or inside out. As, in this method,
it is you who will be inverted, it comes as something of a
relief (though possibly not much) to discover that the idea is
that you will be turned upside down.

―――
*Natural Hair Products Ltd, The Hook, Cedar Road, Woking, Surrey. He has also written a
book, Andy Bryant, *The Baldness Cure* (London: Vermilion, 1994).

No, it's not so that gravity can exercise a greater yank on those follicles and force the hair out! (You're being facetious again, aren't you? Well, please stop it.) The suggestion is that hanging upside down for even a few seconds a day will help the blood flow more easily through those capillaries, packing those nutrients in and taking away all the garbage. There are a couple of ways of doing this.

The first is to bend over. This should be a relatively simple and straightforward process, but, ever conscious of duty to readers, I thought I had better undergo the process on your behalf and see just how difficult it is. Results, after several trials, were conclusive: it *is* a relatively simple and straightforward process!

Why, you may ask, should the ease of this exercise be questioned at all? Simply because NHP will happily supply you with another gizmo, called, ingeniously, an 'inverter', which is a sort of tilting table. It is not to be confused with the only other sort of inverter I have heard of, which converts direct current into indirect. It is not recommended that you attach yourself to one of these and no claims for damage suffered as a result will be considered. NHP's 'inverter', apparently, is finely tuned to provide the correct degree of dilation of the blood vessels. (At about £400 a throw, you might be forgiven for expecting it to wake you up with a cup of tea in the morning as well, but, as far as is known, it doesn't.) As you progress with the course, you spend a little longer 'inverting' until you reach thirty seconds, morning and night.

Among the more esoteric remedies and cure-alls which have appeared over the centuries are cowpats, stale urine, chicken and horse manure, dog-droppings, sheep's afterbirth and God knows what else. Frankly, if you are tempted by any of these, you're on your own (a condition in which, in all probability, you should not be let out). Strange, isn't it, that virtually all these obscure substances which have been advised for application to the head (well, you

didn't think you had to *take* them did you?) are things you
would normally avoid coming into contact with even when
wearing a stout pair of Wellington boots.

Another would-be cure which received some attention a
few years ago was the suggestion that a bald head would
benefit greatly from being licked, daily, by a cow. There is, of
course, no accounting for taste (even that of a cow,
apparently) but, when this one was tried, it was the devil's
own job to get her into the bathroom, let alone keep her
there. Okay, I suppose, if you live on a farm but slightly
impractical for anyone living in a high-rise development.

HERBAL REMEDIES

With the renewed interest in herbal remedies, here are some
rather more acceptable suggestions from Foulsham's reprint
of Culpeper's *Complete Herbal*. Nicholas Culpeper was a
seventeenth-century astrologer-physician and, although the
more astrological aspects of his advice might cause more
amusement than would be seemly to the sceptics, at least the
side-effects of applying herbal solutions are likely to be
limited to a discoloration of the scalp rather than its
removal.

If you feel inclined to heed his recommendations, you
should gather some (or if you are really keen, perhaps all) of
the following: cinquefoil, beets, mouse-ear, walnuts (green,
before the shell forms), yarrow, elm-tree, hound's-tongue,
lily (white), maiden-hair (white), mallows (marsh), though
Culpeper makes no mention of them, we would suggest that
it might be better to avoid the chocolate-covered variety,
mustard (white), peach-tree and thorough-leaf.

It is, of course, essential that you follow Culpeper's
instructions on the preparation of any herbs which you may
choose to try, in which case do refer to his illustrious
volume, but, as a sample of what you may encounter, here is
a little of his advice concerning the use of beets. (He does
suggest that white beet (*beta vulgaris*) is more potent than

red beet (*beta hortesis*), and as he fails to mention pickled beet (*beta vinegaris?*) I would avoid using it.)

Apparently, white beet is governed by Jupiter (so let Jupiter 'be angular and strong' when you gather it) and the relevant extract is as follows:

> It is good for all weals, pustules, blisters and blains in the skin; the herb boiled and laid upon chilblains or kibes, helpeth them: the decoction thereof in water or some vinegar, healeth the itch if bathed therewith and cleanseth the head of dandruff, scurf, and dry scabs, and doth much for running sores, ulcers, and cankers in the head, legs, or other parts, *and is much commended against baldness and shedding the hair.*

Lest you should think that it is hardly worth all the trouble of getting hold of white beet if that's all it can do, he also recommends that this cure-all 'looseneth the belly', 'provoketh the urine', 'openeth obstructions both of the liver and the spleen', and, according to Culpeper, is also just the job for headaches, inflammation in the eyes, turning of the brain and is effective against 'all venomous creatures'. So, if you do use it, be ready for some pretty unpopular and fairly anti-social side-effects.

As a final caution, please note that Culpeper himself, though siring seven children (too much 'asparagus (prickly) for the provocation of lust', perhaps), died of consumption at the age of thirty-eight (presumably, there being no borage, cabbage, horehound or what-have-you to hand).

*

As for the more up to date of the 'miracle cures', 'wonder treatments' and 'hair-stimulant sensations', well, it's up to you, but, as they say, on your own head be it – or, in this case, probably not!

You might even care to try the Elton John technique in which you wear a variety of baseball caps and other headgear for about three years, at the end of which your hair is fully restored. Who knows? At least it's got to be better than putting a cowpat on your head, although, if you finish up looking as though you *have* a cowpat on your head, don't complain to me.

I should just point out one additional fact by way of warning to the easily led. The normal rate of hair growth, at peak, is about 2 cm a month. Any claim to provide you with a full head of hair in eight weeks or so probably means a wig!

Why put yourself through all this trauma and expense?

You are bald and beautiful – enjoy it!

8 more advantages of not having your hair

1 You can never be told to keep it on.

2 Nothing will ever make it stand on end.

3 Other people will no longer be able to get in it.

4 No experience will be capable of raising it.

5 The in-laws will not make you tear it.

6 You will never again turn one.

7 You won't go white overnight.

8 You cannot be accused of splitting them.

But the one-over-the-eight is the good news

9 You can still have one of the dog's if necessary.

British Institute of Bald Awareness

Fellowship Examination – Part 8

Summer 1995

*(The time allowed for this paper is two hours. Candidates are reminded to read every question on the paper, and to answer **all** the questions in Part One of the paper, **six** of the ten questions in Part Two, **four** of the five questions in Part Three and **five** of the three questions in Part Six. Any candidate found reading **Part Four** or **Part Five** of the paper will be asked to leave the examination room and to wear a hairpiece for three months. Answers are to be written on only one side of the paper at a time.)*

Part One

1. Which is the odd one out of the following, and what have the rest in common?

> Avocado; nectarine; star fruit & lemon; guava; water melon & passion fruit; coconut; blackcurrant; mulberry; banana & persimmon; mango & cantaloupe; apple & mint; apple blossom; pawpaw; soap; cherry & lime; apricot; peach & pine nut.

(10 marks)

Chapter 8

THE HAIR-RAISING COST OF HAIR

There's one born every minute.

A cursory glance at the extract from the Summer 1995 fellowship examinations of the British Institute of Bald Awareness will serve as a timely and appropriate introduction to our consideration of the running costs of having the usual full complement of hair.

The answer to the question reproduced from the paper is fairly straightforward. All except one of the items mentioned has been used as a selling point in the alleged contents of hair shampoos or conditioners on public sale. The odd one out is, of course, soap – which, though frequently the basis of the product, hardly ever gets a mention.

This list, by no means either exclusive or exhaustive, shows not, of course, how good all these various fruits may be at chucking nutrients in the general direction of your hair (if in doubt, try rubbing any of them in and see what a mess you get into), but shows rather the expertise and imagination of the marketing men in persuading otherwise rational and sensible members of the general public to part with hard-earned cash in exchange for unnecessary cosmetics for their hair.

Before the current trend for turning any attractive-sounding fruit into a wonder-emulsion for the application to the head, the appearance on the shelves of an 'avocado shampoo' gave rise only to the question, 'Who on earth would want to shampoo an avocado?' Nowadays, in contrast, there would be hardly an eyebrow in the land raised if someone produced a 'strained beef and carrot shampoo' or a 'chicken and prune conditioner'. (Perhaps there is here an innovative marketing opportunity for all those manufacturers of odd-sounding combinations of baby food: simply bung the same old stuff which babies have been spitting out all over kitchens for years in a bottle that would grace the shelves of a bathroom, and, Bob's your uncle, a whole new range of customers emerges.)

It may be that the ever-increasing gush of fruity unguents for the hair is merely an amplification of the current trendy arguments for ecological awareness. The idea being that, subconsciously, as all these things are natural products, the shopping public will believe that having them pouring down the drain will, in some way, do far less damage to the planet than nasty old soap. The fact that most of these products are soap- or detergent-based anyway is, of course, given little or no prominence on the label.

On the other hand, it may also be possible that the cosmetic marketing men are simply following the dictum attributed to Phineas T. Barnum, 'There's a sucker born every minute.'

At a conservative estimate, 98 per cent of the business of the multi-multi-billion-pound perfumery and cosmetics industries is founded upon selling extremely cheap materials at massively inflated prices to people who not only do not need them but who arguably would be better off without them. The success of this huge combine, and we would not say that it is other than *massively* successful, is all the more extraordinary when you consider that it is built on the (always unspoken) implication by the manufacturers that the customer really is not a very attractive person and needs all the help that he or she can get.

To persuade a large proportion of the general populace that they would be improved by putting powdered magnesium silicate and zinc oxide on their faces is quite an achievement, but not as big as making them pay through the nose to do it. Despite that, face powder sells to millions. Millions more, who might conceivably balk at dolloping cocoa butter and lanoline on their mouth, pay fortunes to do so in the guise of lipstick. Those whose chemical ignorance might make them reluctant to step into a bath which they were informed was a solution of borax step with happy heart into the bath salts which Auntie gave them for Christmas – even if they do happen to be the bath salts which they gave Auntie the Christmas before. Cheap plastic on the nails, gum on the eyelashes and heaven knows what else where else, off they stride believing that all this is, in some way doing them good. It may make them feel better – but the cost is astronomic!

The perfume industry alone could be the subject of a life's work for the country's entire army of Fair Trading Officers if the law relating to advertising standards meant anything at all.

Natural perfumes are of animal or vegetable origin and most commercial perfumes are a mixture of the two (either naturally occurring or synthetically reproduced chemical compounds) as the animal perfumes impart a permanence which is lacking in their short-lived vegetable counterparts. There are, apparently, four principal animal perfumes: musk, civet, ambergris and castor and, if the wearers were more aware of the precise sources of these perfumes, they might think rather more than twice about the benefits of wearing them.

Musk is a dried secretion from the foreskin of the musk deer. Civet comes from under the tail of the civet cat (as anyone who has seen one will tell you, not an animal you would ever wish to get closer to than the bars of a cage happily prevent). Ambergris is a secretion of the bile duct of a whale and is alleged only to be produced when the organs are diseased. If you are still with me, or have returned now and are feeling better, castor is not, as you may have fondly imagined (I certainly did), taken from the castor oil plant, but is, more exotically if not attractively, a smoke-dried

glandular secretion of the beaver. (Apparently the secretion is removed from the beaver before smoking.) What delightful sources on which to base an industry whose whole *raison d'être* is the rendering of people more attractive to the nose! Next time you or your partner puts a dab behind the ear, try not to think about that musk deer, or you may have to explain just what has caused you to roll about uncomfortably on the Axminster with a slipper stuffed in your mouth to stifle the laughter.

Now, I admit, that a lot of the above may appear to be a digression from my main thesis, but, if it is, it is only a small one and it has a very definite purpose. You must always remember, whenever you see shelves full of these restorative solutions, emulsions and gallimaufries, all claiming to exercise so much better care for your follicles than those amalgams, fusions and salmagundi to be found on the adjacent shelves, that virtually all of them are products of an industry which is not a million miles away from perfumery and cosmetics. As such, you are likely to be paying heavily over the odds for something which you do not actually need.

Ignore, if you will, and just for a moment, the proliferation of different brands, flavours (well, what would you call them?) and the almost spectrum-wide profusion of colours (certainly available, if not intentionally manu-factured, to match every bathroom colour scheme in the land) under and in which these substances are currently being foisted on the public. Now, cast your mind back to those halcyon days when none but the more sophisticated and specialist stores stocked more than three or four hair shampoos at the most, and consider the sequence of events leading to our present situation. First there came more shampoos, then still more shampoos and then, eventually, even the shampoo marketers realized there was a limit.

Panic! Confusion! Desperation! Then – for these market-ing people – then, inspiration! Persuade everybody that they do not only need shampoo, they need something else as well. Enter – conditioner. For a while, we see the same evolution as we saw with shampoo. New types, colours, ingredients which would make the mouth water – and enough different brands to make the same mouth foam. Next follows catastrophe! Once again, saturation point is reached. The shelves will simply not expand to carry more of the same.

Panic! Confusion! Desperation! Then – for these are still the self-same marketing men – then, not just inspiration, but a stroke of genius. Persuade everybody that they *don't* need shampoo and conditioner. Difficult, of course, as thousands, nay millions, of pounds have just been spent to persuade them that they do.

Enter the marketing spin-doctors. 'Don't tell them they don't need both; tell them that they need something new *which is both!'* Enter the 'two-in-one', 'wash'n'go', 'both-in-the-bottle' – shampoo and conditioner combined. A breakthrough! A masterstroke! A 'quantum leap in the history of hair care.'

It is all part of a never-ending cycle. It's almost guaranteed that, someday very soon, yet another development will ensure that yet another product will be adorning the shelves in the hope that we will all rush to use it to anoint our heads. Vast fortunes will be spent to persuade us that, up to now, our hair has only been partially looked after and that only now, after all their research (pictures of lots of people in white coats – but don't be fooled, marketing consultants can wear white coats too!), can we *really* care for it in the way it should be cared for. Don't fall for it.

Of course, although an appreciable cost, the money paid for shampoos, conditioners and like items is only a part of the expense involved in servicing a full (or partial) head of hair. To this must be added the combs, brushes, haircuts and, by no means least, the *time* spent in the whole process of tonsorial gardening that can occupy a material part of a lifetime.

Chapter 9

GREAT BALD HEROES OF EARLY BRITISH HISTORY

Showing the influence of the bald and (sometimes) the hairy on these fair islands until proper history started in 1066

VERY EARLY DAYS

As the islands emerged from the Ice Age, nothing much of note was happening. People were obviously very hairy at that time because of the climate. Interestingly, one of the first developments was the emergence of a tribe of would-be farmers who grabbed a lot of land in the South of England (as it then wasn't) and began cultivating it. These were known as the Iberians or 'long skulls'. The reason for the name is lost in the mists of time, but they could just possibly have been so-called as a result of being a bald race whose consequently dome-like heads looked, to the poor ignorant 'hairy ones', longer than the average. Nothing much was heard of them later, so they may have been chased out of the land by their envious hirsute rivals. Trevelyan records that there were then only about 700 families in the whole of Southern England (as it then wasn't), so a small force of dedicated men, the equivalent of one busload of Millwall supporters, could have cleared them out in short order.

EARLY DAYS (BUT NOT AS EARLY AS VERY EARLY DAYS)

Baldiciea

The first event of any real historical consequence was the appearance at Deal of the Roman hordes. Gaius Julius Caesar, Emperor of Rome, took it upon himself to invade these islands in 55 BC. It is interesting to speculate as to the effect on world history had Julius Caesar been less concerned with hiding his baldness – just look at the surviving busts. He and the lads had been in Germany and, having become thoroughly bored (the Germans had little sense of fun even in those days), thought he might cheer them up with a cross-Channel trip from Calais to Dover. They opted for the sea crossing and the trip was a disaster. We all know the Italian aptitude for organization, it was often the same even in those days. Too many of the Romans spent too long queueing for duty-frees, and it all ended in chaos and an ignominious return to the mainland.

Caesar returned the following year but this time hardly a Briton showed up on the beach; so Caesar claimed a win and left again. It was nearly another hundred years before Romans returned to the island – though claiming the while that we were part of the Roman Empire – and by then, virtually everybody in Britain had forgotten all about them with the result that the invasion, although meeting pockets of fierce resistance, continued relatively unopposed until it was too late. Unopposed, that is, until AD 61 when the first great heroine of Britain, Baldiciea, came into the picture. There is some dispute amongst scholars as to the name: some allege Boudicca, some Boadicea. We prefer the more likely Baldiciea. Widow of the king of East Anglian Iceni, she was completely bald and described by contemporary historians as 'earnest, rugged and terrible'. Although opinions vary, the word 'rugged' seems almost certainly to refer to her habit of wearing the scalps of those killed in previous battles (i.e. wearing a 'rug' or wig). Baldicea opened

her campaign stunningly well with good wins at Camulodunum (Colchester) and Verulamium (St Allbalds, later corrupted to St Albans) – although the latter victory was helped by St Allbalds' notorious 'sloping pitch', the like of which the Romans had never before encountered, and steady drizzle throughout the match which helped the home side's forward game. Unfortunately, early in the second half, the Romans brought on the very experienced Fourteenth (Pizza Quattro Stagioni) Legion as substitute, and then slipped the veterans of the Twentieth (Mounted Toupee Division) Legion when nobody was looking and, although it went into extra time, it was all over for the Britons. The Romans were through to the next round. Sadly, Baldiciea took umbrage, a particularly virulent form of poison popular in the first century, and died.

The Romans, however (somewhat like their latter-day descendants) were at heart a nation of waiters and hairdressers. They waited for just over 360 years (they were *very* good waiters), but the Ancient Britons, although hairy, were not highly possessed of tonsorial ambition, and never so much as asked for a short back and sides, so having grown tired of waiting, and having more than a little domestic trouble nearer to home, the Romans packed up their pasta makers, their curlers and their hair dryers and left again in AD 410. Nothing much happened for a while after that.

SLIGHTLY LATER DAYS (BUT STILL QUITE EARLY, REALLY)

Plagued by attacks by the Picts, Scots and roving bands of Celtic and Rangers supporters, the British chief, Vortigern, in about AD 450, invited the Saxons over to defend the east coast. As the Saxons were then regarded as the most cruel of all the tribes of Germany, this was an action on a par with seeking pensions advice from Robert Maxwell. Predictably, it had a similar result. The Saxons, under Hengist and

Horsehair, were, like Maxwell, very hairy and not to be trusted. They immediately turned on their hosts and took the land for themselves. At around this time, the legend of King Arthur seems to have sprung up, and although historians are in their usual state of disagreement about the degree of reality behind the myth, very few will dispute that such a chieftain did exist.

King Arthur

The name 'Arthur', according to my researches, was originally from the North of Britain where he was known as Baht'air (without hair) as a result of his complete baldness. On moving to an undocumented part of the West Country (probably somewhere near the Welsh borders), this soon became contracted to Artur or Arthur.

Despite his probable importance to the development of British history, it has to be admitted that little is actually known about Arthur. There is a fairly strong belief that he is the British chieftain who managed to unite various Celtic tribes to repel the Saxon hordes in a famous British victory, probably about AD 500 at an unidentified place called 'Mons Baldonicus' and it seems likely that if this is so, the location ('Mount Bald'un') was named after its hero. It seems highly likely that Arthur was possessed of a strong sense of humour as, in early manuscripts, his court, which the world has come to know as Camelot, the place is referred to as *Comb-alot*, which we believe must be an ironic and self-deprecating allusion to the King's baldness.

NEARLY THE LAST DAYS BEFORE PROPER HISTORY STARTED
(although quite early compared with today)

From the (probable) days of Arthur until the Norman invasion, very little is really known, though it appears that bald men played a not insignificant part in what little history there was.

633   Osbald of Northumbria becomes 'over-king'.
       (Admittedly, some sources refer to Osbald as
       Oswald. Ignore them. I have.)

642   Osbald is killed at Oswestry by Penda (so-called
       because of his long hair) of Mercia.

716   Æthelbald of Mercia becomes King 'not only of the
       Mercians but all of the provinces called by the
       general name Southern English'.

731   The Venerable Bald (some prefer the Old English,
       'Bede' – I don't)

757   Æthelbald, having reigned for 39 years (an almost
       unparalleled length of time in those days), died. As
       a tribute to Æthelbald's success as king, his
       successor took the name Offhair, which was
       subsequently shortened to Offa, and decreed that all
       bald men should not have to pay 'Danegeld'.
       However, as 'Danegeld' did not actually become
       payable until the 990s, this had little impact and is
       seldom referred to in historical works.

796   As a further tribute to Æthelbald, after reigning for
       exactly the same length of time, 39 years, Offa died,
       to be succeeded by our next great bald hero, Alfred.

DEFINITELY THE LAST DAYS BEFORE
PROPER HISTORY STARTED

Alfred the Great
Alfred the Great is almost universally regarded as the king
who saved England against appalling odds. What is not
generally known is that he was actually Alfred the Pate, and
his subsequent, and erroneous, sobriquet came about as a
result of the mumbled dictation of an elderly blind monk to

a particularly dyslexic novice.

His first problem was the Danes. They had come over in 865 and had been roaming about, capturing York, ruling Northumbria, taking over East Anglia and making a general nuisance of themselves without particularly threatening the Southern parts of the land for some years. In 870, however, they camped at Reading and looked set upon taking Wessex. A combined force under King Æthelred and his brother, Alfred the Pate, met them on Berkshire Downs and sent them packing. They withdrew to Reading again, re-packed and defeated the British at Basingstoke which was, even in 871, just as key a marginal as it is today. With the Danes cheating and calling up an additional Danish army, they were poised to invade Wessex. Æthelred died and Alfred took over. Alfred the Pate was a much more skilled manager of troops and, after an initial few battles in which the Danes achieved victories, great tactical commander that he was, he instinctively knew what he had to do to avoid defeat at the hands of the invader – he bought them off and they went to defeat Mercia (Ithsmian League, Division II). Five years later of course, being untrustworthy foreigners, they returned to have another go at Wessex, but their hearts were never really in it and they showed none of the finishing power of the previous touring team, so, this time, the two sides settled for a draw, with the Danes getting that part of the island north of a line roughly from the Wash, down through London up to Chester. This area became known as Danelaw, and, as far as the Britons were concerned, over the next years, the Danelaws were about as popular as the in-laws are today. Danelaw jokes abounded ('How many Danelaws does take to change a wick?') and arguments and minor and major skirmishes continued with them well beyond the end of Alfred the Pate's reign.

Interestingly, the Danes had left one legacy behind them on their forages into the South. A mixture of flour, spices, water and yeast, known as *cakka*, coated in honey, was traditionally used by many Nordic peoples as a reputed cure for baldness. When a number of Alfred's subjects were discovered to be using this mixture, the king, justly proud of his gleaming pate (by which name he was still known) was furious and ordered all the *cakkas* to be burned, giving rise to a wholly unfounded legend which lives under his name to this day. There is a theory which holds that it was the incomplete burning of one batch of *cakkas*, which led to the discovery of what we know today as the 'Danish pastry', but I have been unable properly to verify this and am dubious of its authenticity.

After major contributions to ship-building, education and town-planning (sadly, now, all lost arts in this country) Alfred's end was a sad one. The year was 899, and he finally died of a fit of impatience with all the arguments raging on his Millennium Committee as to whether the celebrations should be held in 900 or 1000 for, despite all Arthur's advances in education policy, mathematics was still in its infancy.

After Alfred's death, he was succeeded by a series of much hairier kings who, quite frankly, would not have been able to tell one end of a kingdom from the other, and it comes as little surprise to discover that just over a hundred years after his death, by 1016, the whole country was under the rule of one sovereign, a Dane. His name was Curlinut, and, though the reasons for it were obvious, he decided, in the interests of kingly dignity, to shorten it to Cnut.

ABSOLUTELY DEFINITELY THE LAST DAYS BEFORE PROPER HISTORY STARTED

In the wake of Cnut's death, there were several possible claimants to the throne. Several descendants of old dynasties were showing interest, Cnut had a couple of wives with sons and there was every chance of confusion reigning. Fortunately, confusion, a distant relative, on his mother's side, of Eric Bloodaxe, one-time king of York, was ruled out as his name did not start with a capital letter. (It was widely thought, at the time, that to have a king whose name was entirely in lower case letters would make England the laughing-stock of the known world.) In the event, one of Cnut's sons, a particularly hairy individual glorying in the name of Hearthrug-Curlinut (known to *some* historians as Harthacnut) decided the question by the simple expedient of changing his name to Cnut and hoping nobody would notice that the king had changed. They didn't.

From then until the accession of Harold, Cnut II (as, eventually, he admitted to being) was followed by a (mostly disputed) succession of kings including, finally, Edward, son of Æthelred, the old king of Wessex. Edward's name should be reviled in the history of bald heroes of British history, but the truth has seldom before been told.

Absolutely bald from the age of 10, when Edward realized that there was an outside chance of his being considered a successor, and aware that for many years, through the reigns of Cnut and Cnut II, kings of England were notoriously hairy, he went into seclusion for three years and emerged with as extravagant a head of hair as has ever been seen. He claimed for many years to have been 'cured' by a witch and it was not until three years before his death that he admitted to wearing a wig. Although the story itself received scant coverage at the time ('investigative journalism' being in its infancy), and is almost universally omitted from historical works, the fact that historical commentators have always referred to him as Edward 'the Confessor' is an indication of how widely the story has been known.

1066 AND THE START OF PROPER HISTORY

It is a strange quirk of the British character that Brits can look back at an event which marked, arguably, their most comprehensive defeat (and, certainly, their most complete and longest lasting invasion and subjugation) and regard it as a victory, but so is 1066 regarded. It is interesting to speculate on why this may be so. Admittedly, one can regard the events of 1066 as leading to the eventual growth and stability of a nation which carries on to this day (give or take the introduction of a few foreign monarchs who took over by invitation), but this does not wholly explain the apparent rewriting of history. As large a paradox, perhaps, is the fact that the next person whom we laud in our 'Bald Heroes of British History' section should be none other than the Conqueror himself.

William I

William of Normandy may seem an unlikely choice of 'bald hero of Britain', possessed, as he was, of a full head of hair and being, as he was, French. William was however a hero *to* the bald rather than of the bald. Having seen the chaos, tribal infighting and general mayhem to which Britain had been subjected whilst under the rule of various hairy kings, and being an educated man, he resolved to draw up a list of those who could be relied upon in any future crisis. Naturally, he needed men from all over his kingdom, ready in place and known to (and trusted by) the locals, should problems arise. To this effect, he sent envoys and agents throughout the lands to compile a register of all those on whom he felt he could depend and, though ignored by most historians, a notoriously hairy and baldist elite, it is a fact that all those stout burghers so registered were, to some extent, bald or balding.

Of course, at the time, many noblemen were wearing their hair fashionably long and many showed no signs of baldness whatsoever. It would have been foolhardy for William openly to acknowledge his 'Register of the Bald' and would have been downright stupid to refer to it by some title such as 'Bald People Who Can Be Trusted' for this might well have provoked those not so fortunate to rise up against him. The solution was as simple as it was brilliant. He called it 'The Domes-day Book' in honour of all those domes therein who he was confident would come to his aid.

Chapter 10

TOUPEE OR NOT TOUPEE?

INTERVIEWER: *How long does it take to have your hair done?*
DOLLY PARTON: *I don't know: I'm never there.*

For those men becoming aware that they are soon to be possessed of less than the average standard issue of hair, at some time (if only in their innermost thoughts), as the great bard put into the mouth of the ill-fated Prince of Denmark, 'toupee or not toupee?' is indeed the question.

The rest of the speech in the first draft of *Hamlet* is:

> Toupee, or not toupee: that is the question:
> Whether 'tis nobler for the head to suffer
> The slings and arrows of outrageous slander,
> Or to don hair against a sea of insults,
> And by so wearing end them? To wear? To bare
> No more; and buy a wig to say we end
> The heart-ache and the thousand barb'd remarks
> Bare scalp is heir to, 'tis a consummation
> Devoutly to be wish'd.

How well he understood! Indeed, by a cursory glance at any of the contemporary pictorial representations of the old boy, how well he knew. Of course, he changed the text a little on rewriting (you might have been tempted to do the same if your queen was as bald as a coot with little or no sense of humour and a penchant for a range of punishments in which being bound over to keep the peace did not feature too largely) but the original lines have a relevance even today to those who are still ashamed or embarrassed at their baldness. How tiresome those 'slings and arrows' that even family and friends can propel towards us, and how tempting it must be to buy that wig and don that hair and end the barbed remarks?

Resist, good friends, resist. As this book tries to show, there are other, better, ways of opposing those 'slings and arrows' than by the purchase, at no small expense, of something which, at best, will be reminiscent of a small rodent that has had an embarrassing experience with a heavy roller and which, at worst, may look like the same mammal dead from a particularly wasting disease which left it permanently deformed.

The Ancient Egyptians may have started it all. Being relatively civilized men, they realized the uselessness of hair even then and used to shave their heads, but then went and spoilt it all by wearing those short black bob-style wigs which in those ancient drawings and portraits make them all look like Elizabeth Taylor. The major force in the introduction of wigs as a fashion accessory was the court of Louis XIII of France, the first of the Bourbons, in the seventeenth century. Louis was bald and, presumably, his court was full of those uncivilized baldist types who find it tirelessly amusing to poke fun at the less hirsute. (Interesting to speculate that had the guillotine been invented just 150 years earlier, by now baldness might have been completely accepted.) As a result, he took to wearing wigs and the fashion spread throughout Europe. It might well have died out, of course, but Louis XIII was followed by his son, innovatively called Louis XIV, who, although possessed of a full head of hair, decided to continue the practice for the extraordinary reason that he was so short it would give him added height! As he must have known that all the courtiers would have (as courtiers have through the ages even unto today) passed their exams in toadying with flying colours, and would thus immediately follow the fashion like so many courtly sheep, the height advantage must have been minimized.

Thus was the fashion for wigs born and it continued to develop throughout this period until men were wearing creations of such advanced engineering on their heads that their 'hair' grew ludicrously out of all proportion to both their heads and their bodies and must have given the French court a hilarious similarity to Ladies' Day at Royal Ascot. Presumably, the fashion developed up to the point where both men's and women's centres of gravity had become inconsistent with standing up and they all started toppling over in a rather unbecoming manner. For whatever reasons, in the eighteenth century, wigs became smaller and people started powdering them so that everyone looked as if suffering permanently from terminal dandruff.

Is all this really an attitude which we wish to see carried on today? At least at the court of France, the wigs were genuine fashion statements; a dubious attribute at best, but not something which can be advanced in defence of all the flattened hedgehogs which are worn today.

Look at those wig-wearing men that you see about you, poor, sad creatures that they are. Consider what goes through your mind as you 'look for the join' or (dare I suggest) as you wonder what the effects of a high wind might be on their tonsorial monstrosity. Could you really live with the knowledge that people were having such thoughts about you? Could you bear the strain of wondering if, indeed, the 'join' is visible, of eternal worrying about the effects of that self-same wind?

Imagine the damage to your life-style. No more could the impulsive deed, the unconstrained act of the moment, feature in your day – or night. Every thought, every action, almost every breath would be fraught with danger: the danger of exposure. That any man should regard the exposure of a balding pate to be unacceptable and yet prefer to live constantly with the threat of far worse, the exposure of a balding pate badly hidden by an object which resembles something brought in by the cat (if not the cat itself), is completely unimaginable to the sane mind.

Think of those elements of your everyday routine which

would immediately be transformed into minefields of doubt and reservoirs of uncertainty. The shower would gush with dangers to all but the most securely fastened; the donning and doffing of a hat would involve a degree of precision out of all proportion with the basic task itself; sleep would come only fitfully as the half-shut eye was startled by a stranger within the room, only to discover your furry friend resting, immobile, on its featureless block. No more the swimming trip with friends, no more the walks upon the blasted heath, no more the pleasant social game of cricket upon the village green. Each of these would be anathema.

What if, diving in, you strike out manfully for the opposite bank only to espy your hair swimming in the opposite direction? Or, at last, on achieving the summit of the hill, what if a rogue gust should propel your hirsute appendage into a neighbouring county? Or what if you painstakingly battle your way, one lazy afternoon, on some treacherous 'sticky dog' of a wicket, to the fifty which will save your team from the jaws of defeat, only to have the taste of victory turn to ashes (admittedly, the nearest to 'Ashes' that an English cricketer is likely to get these days) in your mouth as, casually raising your cap modestly to acknowledge the cheers of the throng, you casually raise your hair as well? Strong of character is the man who could face any of these with equanimity and serenity of soul.

Actually, he is not so much strong of character as bloody daft! As St Mark wrote, 'What shall it profit a man, if he shall gain the whole world, and lose his soul?' – but for a wig!

If, after all this, you are *still* not convinced of the sheer senselessness and the absurd inanity of wearing a rolled rat on your head, if you refuse to demur at the prospect of concealing your crowning glory with a small colony of *someone else's* dead hair, if you are still tempted to part with great wads of the happy-cabbage in order to make yourself look like a walking advertisement for some small-scale taxidermist, then there really is very little hope of converting you.

As a last attempt to divert you from wigdom, we should

just ask you to reflect on romantic moments. There are very few women who can manage to keep an entirely straight face, when, having run their fingers affectionately through a man's hair, the hair decides to dissociate itself from his head. Unusual is the passion that can withstand, at a vital moment, the apparent revelation that one's partner comes with unforeseen removable extras.

One of the few *completely* honest advertisements which we have ever seen for wigs and hairpieces contained the memorable line:

Bald? We can change your life!

10 things your wig may be called
1   Piece
2   Rug
3   Irish
4   Toop
5   Lid
6   Cowpat
7   Divot
8   Door mat
9   Top
10   Muff
Are you sure you still want to wear one?

Chapter 11

POLITICS: THE BALD TRUTH

It ain't by princerples nor men
My preudunt course is steadied
I scent which pays the best, and then
Go into it baldheaded.

James Russell Lowell
The Biglow Papers (1848)

There have, over the years, been many conspiracy theories with political bases, and many fortunes have been made both from the conspiracies themselves and, much more often (and, generally, much more lucratively) from the whole libraries of books and their various spin-off films, television programmes, part-works, and even tee-shirts, baseball caps, etc. Although there is not so much as a merchandised bookmark to back up this theory, it is obvious that one of the biggest world-wide political conspiracies revolves around baldness.

Despite that fairly widespread, and very unattractive, British pastime of denigrating our one-time heroes, *most* objective opinions (other than those with a book to sell or a name to make) would rank Winston Churchill, certainly during his wartime administration, as the greatest Prime Minister the nation ever had. Of course, there are those who claim that, through every minute of the war, he was too drunk to run a post office let alone a country, or that he was just a warmonger who should have done a deal with Hitler,

or even (mark our words, this one will emerge just as soon
as all other avenues of controversial opinion about the great
man as a route to a healthy bank balance have been
exhausted) that he *did* do a deal with Hitler and the
holocaust was all his idea. But as I have stated, to objective
opinion, he was possibly the greatest hero that the country
has known. He was also almost completely bald.

He was followed by Clement Attlee, another member of
that illustrious band. After that, at the time of writing,
Britain's Prime Ministers have possessed at least more than
the average amount of hair with only one exception. Eden,
Macmillan, Wilson, Heath, Callaghan, Thatcher (significantly, perhaps, the hairiest of the lot) and Major, all, at the
time of their premiership, were possessed of what is
laughably known as a healthy head of hair. The only
exception, and a very short-lived one at that, was Alec
Douglas-Home, to whom I shall return later. Is it a mere
coincidence then that, since those days, Britain has seen a
steady decline as a world power? I think not.

But the conspiracy may not be restricted to these islands.
If we should look at America, we have to go back to
Eisenhower to find a man with a reasonably presentable
head. Since Dwight, they have had Kennedy, Johnson (not
over-hirsute, but originally only elected to the position by
Lee Harvey Oswald, and arguably then proving to be one of
America's best in recent years), Nixon (how hairy can a man
get!) Ford (OK, we're not saying that *every* bald man can be
a genius), Carter, Reagan (odd colour but plenty of it!), Bush
and now Hillary Clinton (who between the two of them have
more hair than the others put together).

Why has this happened? Surely, it is too consistent a
happening to be put down to coincidence. If we consider the
rest of Europe through this period we find stalwarts (judged
in the eyes of their own country's interests) as De Gaulle and
Adenauer, and now Kohl and Chirac, much more
acceptably-headed, and leading their nations with a greater
degree of sure-footedness than has been evident in either
America or Britain over a comparable time.

Nevertheless, it appears that at some time very early in the second half of the twentieth century, public opinion was shaped to believe that, to be successful, a man should have as near a full head of hair as is possible. When one contemplates the deeds of those with full heads of hair even in recent history, this may be hard to believe, and certainly, in years to come, when the century becomes reviewed with proper historical perspective, it may be quite impossible for future generations to comprehend. This is, after all, the century in which hairy men have wrought more damage to the world than any other.

Consider this prodigiously hairy list: Joseph Stalin, Adolf Hitler (as well as Goering, Goebbels and virtually the entire High Command of the Third Reich, not excluding such charming hangers-on as Dr Mengele and his team), Hirohito of Japan, Ceausescu of Romania ... The list grows right up through Saddam Hussein (and his twenty-odd doubles) to the present mob of thugs arguing over who should get Bosnia – should any of it be left after they have finished tearing it and its population to bits.

So when did the 'outlawing of the bald man as leader' become the generally accepted norm? Let us go back to Alec Douglas-Home for a moment.

Alec Douglas-Home was a man who is generally agreed to have been one of the country's best regarded Foreign Secretaries. Although passed the job of Prime Minister by (hairy) Macmillan largely because he didn't want to give it to (completely bald) Butler, Douglas-Home (mainly because of the short length of time before an election had to be called and the state to which Macmillan had reduced the government by the time of the hand-over) had precious little time in which to recover anyway, but he is widely thought, by political commentators, to have been the first Prime Minister to lose an election *because of his appearance*.

This, of course, was in the sixties, that decade already referred to when hair growth reached its fashionable worst. It was fast becoming the era of the common man and the fourteenth Earl of Home (as he had been before Macmillan dropped him in it), with his aristocratic appearance and balding pate, simply did not fit in with the requirements of public opinion. (In all probability, the government was then in such a parlous state that, had it been led by all four Beatles and Adonis himself, it would have been unelectable.) So ended the last British premiership of a man with an acceptable head of skin, and so entered the years of the hairy.

Currently, the omens for Britain are even worse. Consider for a moment those whose wives may, even as we write, be spending their resting hours thumbing through the Osborne & Little wallpaper books and harbouring thoughts of calling in the removal men to transport them to Number 10.

From the Conservative party: Heseltine (whose mane seems to increase in direct proportion to his chances of getting there). Portillo (who even sports a quiff for Heaven's sake!), Clarke, even, possibly (the thoughts don't have to be realistic). Lamont? The Labour party is currently led by Blair, with Brown, Prescott and Cook in close pursuit. The Social Democrats have the nerve to offer us Ashdown. Hairy to a man, and, although a week in politics may be a long time, there must be a fair chance, unless this loathsome tide can be reversed, that those lists could well contain a combination of Britain's Prime Ministers for the next thirty years! By that time, the country could have had hirsute leaders for sixty-five years, and who knows what parlous state we may have achieved by then.

So what can be done? More accurately and constructively, you may be asking, 'What can *I* do?'

First, irrespective of your party allegiance and without regard for your possible lack of interest in any form of politics, campaign in local and national elections for the selection of bald candidates. Irrespective of under whichever banner the candidates may be fighting (as if, in the long run, it ever makes any difference anyway) decide to vote for the candidate with least hair.

If you have the energy and the funds (both of which will be required in enormous amounts) form your own party, call it something catchy such as 'Baldies For Britain', choose a winning slogan along the lines of 'A Smooth Future' or 'Win With Skin' (as will have been seen by example, they don't actually have to mean anything) and fight to regain the ground that the image-makers have taken from us.

If these faceless people continue to shape the form of 'acceptable man' for much longer, we will be confronted by a future in which the nation will be led by a never-ending series of outstanding coiffeured heads atop wondrously tailored suits, and, by the time that we all realize that there is nothing inside either the suits or the heads, it may be too late to fight back.

Write an anthem for your new political party with the title:

'Be Bald For Britain
And
Make Her Great Again'

Chapter 12

SOME LITERARY ENCOURAGEMENT

There are some one hundred and ninety-three living species of monkeys and apes. One hundred and ninety-two of them are covered in hair. The exception is a naked ape self-named Homo sapiens.

Desmond Morris
The Naked Ape (1967)

When as great an authority on human and animal behaviour as Desmond Morris speaks thus, albeit roughly thirty years ago, it ill behoves me to argue. It also ill behoves anyone else to impute other than objective motives to such an illustrious scholar and gentleman, merely because he happens to be deficient (we would, of course, say laudably deficient) in the follicle region himself. No, the implication was, and is, there for all to see – man is now to be regarded *as an animal without hair*.

However, not even Desmond Morris can hope completely to overcome decades – or perhaps millennia – of prejudice in a mere thirty years of publication, particularly as there is litererary evidence of the awareness of the desirability of the smooth and shining surface dating from earlier. Yet it too, has apparently failed similarly.

From the Good Book onwards there are many exhortations to the depilated state.

'Behold, Esau my brother is a hairy man, and I am a smooth man.' (Genesis, ch.27, v.11). So, the Old Testament informs us, spake Jacob, as, in this case, the hairy man's only lasting claim to fame has been the signally unintelligent decision to sell his birthright for a bowl of lentil soup, whereas the smooth one went on to sire the patriarchs of the twelve tribes of Israel, there I might well rest my case.

Later there is also a very instructive tale warning against the perils of insulting the bald-headed, which should be heeded by all would-be perpetrators of baldness abuse.

> And he (Elisha) went up from thence unto Beth-el; and as he was going up by the way, there came forth little children out of the city, and mocked him, and said unto him, Go up, thou bald head; go up, thou bald head. And he turned back, and looked on them, and cursed them in the name of the LORD. And there came forth two she bears out of the wood, and tare forty and two children of them.
>
> II Kings, ch.2, vv.23–4

Yes, well, obviously, the chances of the appearance of 'two she bears out of the wood', if you happen to find yourself in, say, the saloon bar of the Pig and Oboe in Chalfont St Giles, may be somewhat remote, but you get the picture. (You might even carry the reference around in case you are abused by a reverend gentleman with a less than Christian attitude to his fellow man.)

St Paul was quite definite about it: 'Doth not even nature itself teach you, that if a man have long hair, it is a shame unto him?' (I Corinthians ch.11, v.14, To put to rest the minds of our female readers, we should add that the quotation continues: 'But if a woman have long hair, it is a glory to her.'

What could be clearer than that?

The world of more temporal literature is also liberally sprinkled with references to gladden the hearts of the glabrous. (This attractive term, from the Latin *glaber* – hairless, is normally biological or technical, but deserves wider use.)

John Ford, the seventeenth-century English playwright, wrote in 1633 in act 4, scene 2 of his *The Broken Heart*:

> There's not a hair
> Sticks on my head but, like a leaden plummet,
> It sinks me to the grave:

More recently, in 'The Scholars', W.B. Yeats wrote of 'Old, learned, respectable bald heads' (not sure about the old, but the 'learned' and 'respectable' seem reasonable enough) and more recently still, we are indebted to Fred Astaire's biographer, Bob Thomas, for unearthing a rash American film studio official's comment which could be a salutary lesson for those tempted into baldism but unaware of its dangers. His comment on an early Astaire screen test? 'Can't act. Slightly bald. Can dance a little.' As Astaire's film career developed rather more than might have been expected from that, cricket aficionados might regard it as akin to saying of Don Bradman, 'Can't bowl. Slightly bald. Also bats.'

You may well be asking, and not unreasonably perhaps, 'Well, if all these learned authorities have failed to change the attitude to baldness, what chance do you stand?' Come, come, dear readers, is that the spirit which made this country Great? Is that the attitude of Drake, Raleigh and Churchill?

To fail may lead a fellow to despair, but not as surely as to fail to dare.

Let us leave the final words to scholar and lyricist, A.E. Housman, perhaps most famous for 'A Shropshire Lad'.
   Here then, a cautionary tale on the dangers of hair:

> Oh who is that young sinner with the handcuffs on
>   his wrists?
> And what has he been after that they groan and shake

their fists?
And wherefore is he wearing such a conscious-stricken
  air?
Oh they're taking him to prison for the colour of his
  hair.
'Tis a shame to human nature, such a head of hair as
  his;
In the good old time 'twas hanging for the colour that
  is his;
Though hanging isn't bad enough and flaying would be
  fair
For the nameless and abominable colour of his hair.

How much better he would have fared if he had had none at
all!

Appendix

WHALEY'S BALD MOVIE GUIDE

A comprehensive guide to forthcoming theatrical and video releases

THEATRICAL RELEASES

FOUR STYLINGS AND A HAIRCUT (18)

Starring: Hugh Grant, Elizabeth Hurley and a host of 'Oh-that's-the-bloke-from-whassaname type stars'.

Peter Willow (Hugh Grant) is one half of the first ever pair of mixed-sex Siamese twins and, roguishly attractive as ever, needless to say very popular with women but amazingly self-effacing about it. At least he would be if it wasn't for his twin sister, Petra (Elizabeth Hurley, here seen continuously at his side *throughout* the film, rather than just at the premières and award ceremonies for obvious reasons). Petra is deeply jealous of Peter's success in almost everything he turns his hand to (they each have only the one, as they are, unusually, joined at the wrist) and in her constant quest for attention, tries four different hairstyles, before finding the one which seems to work. At last, the world is looking at her, but Peter has other ideas, and in a hilarious end scene (which will be, unfortunately but undoubtedly, the one which everyone will have seen in the clips before going to see the film) he decides to have his head shaved completely and steal the limelight once again.

93 minutes

A WIG CALLED WANDA (PG)

Starring: John Cleese, Jamie Lee Curtis, Michael Palin and Kevin Kline.

Pendlebury Waddington (John Cleese) is a High Court judge who has three problems. They are that he is starved of affection, aware that he is getting older, balding, and cannot come to terms with any one of them. In the belief that it will cure all three, he secretly buys a hairpiece and so that he will not be found out, the wigmaker and he refer to the piece as Wanda in all their dealings. At first, Pendlebury is so embarrassed by his wig that the will only wear Wanda under his judicial wig, which does rather limit its effect, but, one day hurrying to re-robe himself for the afternoon session at the Old Bailey, after a particularly exhausting lunch, he hilariously wears Wanda on top of his official wig. Enter Harriet Farmer, known as Harry and played by Jamie Lee Curtis, who is a small-time American confidence trickster who has been trading (fraudulently) as a trichologist. Pendlebury completely loses his marbles, but, thanks to his being a High Court judge, nobody notices and their adventures begin.

8 hours!

THE WIG (NG)

Starring: Jim Carrie and nobody anyone else has heard of this side of the Atlantic.

Yes, Jim Carrie is back in a brand new film with all the appeal of the box-office bursting success of 'The Mask', but with a breathtakingly different concept and storyline. A young, balding insurance clerk (Jim Carrie) is bored with his humdrum life and seeks excitement. Partly in his quest to change his personality, but mostly for a joke, he buys a toupee and takes it home where he leaves it in a drawer. One evening, alone (apart from his cute, and highly photogenic, Jack Russell terrier) in his apartment, he decides to try it on and, being made from native hair from an unknown African village, the magical properties in the wig completely transform him into an animated figure with the superhuman attributes of a cartoon character. Unfortunately, a couple of days later, the Jack Russell encounters the wig lying on a chair and attacks it thinking it to be a rat. In the scuffle, the wig lands (hilariously) on the dog's head and turns him into a cartoon dog. Realizing that he can now do anything, the dog jumps from the tenth-floor window into the street below but, before he hits the ground, a gust of wind blows the wig off his head and he reverts to a dog some 120 feet before he hits the ground with the inevitable result that the film is surprisingly short.

16 minutes

VIDEO RELEASES
(all available for sale or rental)

HONEY, I'VE SHRUNK THE WIGS (U)

Eccentric inventor mistakenly reduces the size of her husband's enormous selection of wigs by programming the wrong washing cycle on her washing machine.

STAR WIGS 23 (PG)

Yet another unlikely group of aliens threaten to graft hair onto all the balding people on earth in an effort to take over the universe. From the same team which brought you the previous 22 'Star Wigs' films (and largely made up of out-takes from all of them) they're still all 'baldly going where no man has been before – the big question is 'Why?'

PERMINATOR 4 (PG)

Arnold Schwarzenegger (or is it Sylvester Stallone, I can never remember, even when I'm watching them) is back waging his one-man war against the forces of darkness who, this time, want compulsory permanent waving on all American males over 25.

DYE HARD 7 (18)

Bruce Willis's all-action hero returns to save a thriving, ultra-modern American city from the menace of a crack Eastern European team of hair terrorists who are threatening to poison the city's stock of hair colourants. (Or should I say 'colorants'?)

HOWARD'S RUG (U)

Another truly beautiful film from Merchant Ivory, shot entirely on location in India. Quite why this should be, when the little-known E.M. Forster novella on which it is based was set in Letchworth, remains a mystery.

RESERVOIR WIGS (18)

Quentin Tarantino pulls it off again, as do many of the characters in this fast-moving, undeniably violent, action adventure in which a group of bald vigilantes take positive discrimination further than ever before as they rid the world of toupee wearers.

VIDEO CLASSICS
(NEW ISSUES RELEASED IN TIME FOR CHRISTMAS)

ON THE BLEACH (18)

Starring: Gregory Peck, Ava Gardner, Fred Astaire.

With the world devastated by an atomic war which has bleached the hair of all the survivors possessed of the stuff, a team of bald scientists (led by Fred Astaire) sets out in a submarine to determine if any intelligent life has been spared.

GONE WITH THE WIND (U)

Entire rain forests have been felled, merely to provide the paper for the books about the 1939 MGM classic starring Clark Gable and Vivien Leigh and its story of the egotistical Scarlett O'Hara who survives the Civil War in the deep South only to lose the man she loves. Unfortunately, this isn't it. This one stars Jack Warner and Elsie and Doris Waters, and is a story of two sisters who hang out their bald brother's wig to dry on a very windy day with significantly less than hilarious results.

RUGGY

Starring: Sylvester Stallone (or is it Arnold Schwarzenegger?) Burgess Meredith.

Dim-witted boxer from Philadelphia becomes a laughing-stock by trying to win the Heavyweight Championship whilst wearing a hairpiece. To paraphrase W.C. Fields's reputed death-bed confession ('On the whole. I'd rather be in Philadelphia'), on the whole, we'd rather be dead.

THE MALTESE HAIRPIECE

Starring: Humphrey Bogart, Mary Astor, Sydney Greenstreet, Peter Lorre.

Written and directed by John Huston, from Dashiel Hammett's novel, this classic masterpiece traces the quest for a priceless toupee which follows the death of Sam Spade's partner.

HOW GREEN WAS MY TOUPEE

Starring: Walter Pidgeon, Maureen O'Hara, Roddy McDowell.

After the Hollywood milestone which was 'How Green Was My Valley', the studios turned to Richard Llewellyn's earlier, but mostly forgotten, novel for this story evoking childhood memories of life in a Welsh wig-manufacturing village.

WIGADOON

Starring: Gene Kelly, Cyd Charisse, Van Johnson.

A couple of Americans travelling in Scotland stumble across a sleepy village which only awakes every one hundred years in order to supply the country with wigs made from concentrated haggis. They sing a lot (the Americans, not the wigs).